I0441166

Sell Your Dreams

The science of writing novels and non-fiction, to write them fast, edit them fast, publish and get maximum money into your own pocket.

By Corrie Lamprecht

This book is a compilation of the four
eBooks that formed the series.

Thank you for considering this Book.

I trust this book will be a great help in achieving your dreams to write you own books and successfully market them.

To my Friends

Hilton

Who always nagged me "You have to write a book". Maybe, because he always fell asleep when I am just warming up?

Then he said, "*I feel like shaking you, get to the point!*"

Thank you Hilton, your support is much appreciated.

Banks

If it were not for your insight and support, I would never have tried to writing again. Always ready to record whatever I am talking! Thank you Banks, for you pushing me into this turmoil. I hope your love life will not take you away from writing too long.

Louis

Up in Chiang Rai is a matchmaker... Thank you for accommodating me, and the introductions to interesting people. I hope you enjoy the beautiful mountains for a very long time.

Boonta

Every day she asks, *"How many books you sold?"* Better support and motivation I could not ask for. May all your dreams come to be true. Wish you only happiness.

What if you can write your book and never experience a writer's block? Learn how to structure your book and how to make a very good outline. Generate thousands of variations for your stories. Writing successful books is not just typing many words in strings; it is a science. You will find many tips and tricks in this book. You want a good story; you want to write a solid based non-fiction book? This book will set you off on a path not followed by many – a path that cannot fail in making you an Author.

Spend two or three days to create failsafe outline. Then let it lose and write your story. Even if you cannot type fast, 20,000-words a day is easy. The minimum editing afterwards, and done. Get on with the next book in no time. This book presents you with a few of the more traditional methods, and less than traditional - and explains how to apply them.

Are you experiencing 'Writers Block' or your BIG story ending after few pages? In this book, you will learn the ultimate system for outlining your planed book, and never get a pre-mature dead book on your computer again.

Failsafe story lines, fast writing, fast typing and guidance on getting your book to the market, and maximum royalties back into your own pocket.

This book is a compendium of the four books published in the series "Sell Your Dreams".

Index.

Sell Your Dreams
Science of Writing

Corrie Lamprecht

PART 1 – Writing Fiction.

Ever since humankind lives on this planet, we had the desire to tell stories, and to listen to the stories. Our ancestors sat in the evening around the campfire telling about their ancestors, about the stories in the stars, and about the creatures they met in their lives. Although these were just stories, or history, or myths - mostly it served to educate.

Today we still tell stories. We write them in poetry, write books, make movies and create drawings. Storytelling is still similar to that of the past millennia. A good story always had at least four clear elements – characters, scenery, climax and resolution. These we can still see today in all of the myths, even in astronomy.

In this book, you might find there are statements, which seems to contradict the general accepted norms. They are actually a paradox. Where you find most people shape their books according to the rule of Main Character vs The Opposition; that is good, but it is sometimes incomplete. Apply the three rule. Funny that one of the most successful genre is romance and the best amongst them are usually a love triangle. On the other hand, you can write a whole novel about only one person – with inner conflict.

We as humans have three main purposes in our life. Our first duty is to gain knowledge, our second to reproduce and finally we have to pass the knowledge on to the next generation. These three aspects are encoded in our genes - Knowledge, Reproduction and Education. That will propel humankind to new heights in the future. That is why most people have the urge to create art – which includes the writing of books.

Within the field of drawing art, developments were from cave wall paintings to canvas painting, that could be transported, and now electronic art, which is instantaneously available all over the world. We have the same in writing. The first forms or storytelling was only verbal around the campfires. From there it developed into rock paintings, clay tablet writings, and books – now we are in the Electronic age.

There were also great improvements, mostly due to competition. More people compete for the attention (and money) from more other people. In fact, it is stupid for me to even write this book. Why should I share this precious understanding and system with you? To create more competition for myself in an already very competitive world? That is me, here I am and here you are. I do pamper my 'conscious mind' in the knowledge that it is very unlikely that many people will read this book, and of those – most will not do the effort to follow this understanding.

That is the one warning. If you are looking for the easy magic wand to create your bestseller book – better go to Fiver.com or the likes where you can pay a Ghostwriter, to write it on your behalf. If you want to write your own books, it is going to take a lot of work and a lot of learning. This is my way, the road I prefer to walk on. I can proudly say, *"Every book or article I ever wrote was my own creation. It is my own words formed by my own hand."* That is satisfaction and happiness – never mind if the book is a top seller or just sold one copy. It is me, and it is my piece of art.

There is no magic abracadabra for writing. Letter for letter, word for word you will have to work on it. Luckily, we live in a magical modern age. We do not need to type every letter anymore. In fact, as I explained in a later chapter "Writing Fast" – you can write a 20,000-word book in one single day, even if you cannot type. Then we have the wonderful things like spelling and grammar checkers to make sure our books are not too horrible. We do not need to beg a publisher anymore. Publication of our books is guaranteed. Available for purchase throughout the whole world, in a matter of hours after we decided it is finished.

That is the easy part. The difficult comes in with the writing. How to structure your book to make sure readers wants to read it? Unlike the old days, people are more sophisticated. They read because they want to learn, yes. More so, people read because, for a short period, they want to escape on a magical trip. While there is no magic to write your book – you book have to be the magic for the reader.

Your book needs to be structured. Not only is it an Art anymore – it is also a science. In this book, I will try my best to convey the Science of the writing process. You will use this to create your art.

With this system, the concept of "Writers Block" is not going to happen. You will create your story, you will write it and you will complete it. Blank screens will not be part of your problem.

My Story, My Writers Block.

I had a great idea for a story. Got to my computer before sunrise and made a short outline of my story. Then I thought about the three main sections – Introduction, main body, conclusion. I started writing. Three pages and some 1,200 words later, the flow was over. I just sat there, staring at the screen. My story is finished. I lost it. There is not enough to publish a book! I made breakfast, came back to the computer and stare at the screen. I just could not figure out what to write more. I read, edited, re-read, re-edited – but the story was dead, the word count remains at 754.

The next day I looked at my great idea. I just do not know what to write anymore. I started a new book. This one I was going to be a bit more structured – I defined my main character in nice details, a specialist banker. Then I started writing how he got a message, on to the plane to Brazil and . . . I was stuck after three pages. I found myself falling over the cliff into a Writers Abyss. Again. What is wrong with me? I did write a number of non-fiction books. It seems I am destined to keep on writing non-fiction – always dreaming of becoming a great fiction writer. I want to write fiction books, with a tint of the non-fiction real world in them – and unexpected twists in the story lines. *"No boring stuff from my hand."* Yet, here I am like a warship with no engine – floating dead on the great ocean.

I know my English language skills are not the best, but the same thing even happens when I try to write in Afrikaans. I started following a number of writing courses. I even completed two online courses from Universities. I am talking of maybe 600 hours in total. I have watched more than 100 videos – but the magic is not coming through.

Hey, everybody say you must have to outline your story. OK, I set off with that idea, the same as I do with my non-fiction and articles. Introduction, body, conclusion. I succeeded in taking my few fiction attempts to three or four pages. Then the 'Blank Screen' hits me, again - time after time. They even have a nice word for it, 'Writers Block'.

I am not one that easily gives up on something I want to do. Rather the opposite, I will keep on trying, even to the point of self-destruction. I kept on learning, watching videos and trying. The problem is not about the idea or concept or storyline – that I do have plenty in supply. It is just that everything seems to peter out before it can bloom. It is like a flowering plant with no fertilizer.

Eventually, I found my answers – now I am a free flying, word-spitting dragon.

I challenge you to make your writing a form of Art. Writing a book is a wonderful experience. Even if you finish and publish your book; and nobody buys it. The great feeling is in your heart. "*I did it. This is my creation.*" It does not matter whether you are writing a Fiction or Non-fiction. Unless you express it in your own creative way, it is just going to be another 'document'.

What exactly is art? "*Art is the expression or application of human creative skill and imagination, typically in a visual form such as painting or sculpture, producing works to be appreciated primarily for their beauty or emotional power.*" We know of art as paintings and sculptures, music and photography. Writing is definitely another form of art.

When you come to writing fiction, nearly all laws about writing should be out the window. A good fiction novel is you placing your heart and your mind into words. It is your own creative mind, your own style. Forget the laws! If it is your style to say "You is in trouble" rather than "You are in trouble" then that is YOU. You can rightfully claim your 'Creative Form of Art'. Basta, with all the others and their silly laws; if it is your style to say "*How'dy*" rather than "*Good Morning. How are you?*" then that is perfect. It shows character.

There is one big important law in writing fiction. *Make your reader part of your book, let them feel they are right there – inside your book.* Until recently, I was still set in my old school mind of writing the way my English Teacher always wished me to do. Perfect English, edited hundreds of times, proofread by professional English, et al. However, when I read my first book I did not 'feel it' anymore. So what went wrong? I lost my creative writing, again. I spend months now doing research about who write in what way. Whom would I like to use as a role model? What kind of fiction would I like to write?

Allow me to share with you one of the most amazing findings. There is an interesting phenomenon. I looked through a few lists the likes of 'Greatest books' and '100 Best books of the 21st century'. Not one of them lists any of the Harry Potter series and amongst various Best Authors lists – only one had J.K Rowling as best-seller author. I wonder why?

I think the answer lies right there in the beginning of her writing career. Jo Rowling was a jobless divorced single parent English teacher, living on low budget in Scotland with diagnosed clinical depression. That was after her time as Foreign Language English teacher stint in Portugal where she met, married, conceived and divorced her husband within a record-breaking time of about 14 months. Her first novel was presented to twelve publishing houses in 1995. That was still the old ways when writing took many months, then print the book in paper format and slap your shoes down the road to publishing houses. All rejected. The one, which she has a post of the letter on her website, even claimed that she should first go to learn English and then rewrite the book.

Eventually Bloomsbury accepted to publish the book, though her agent advised Jo Rowling to get a day job. She would not be able to make a living from writing children's fiction.

Presently, J.K. Rowling has sold more than 400 million book copies, with that first rejected book as the fourth bestseller book in all of history. A whooping 107-million copies. J.K. Rowling moved up from welfare benefits and a state of "*poor as it is possible to be in modern Britain, without being homeless.*" to be the 12th richest woman in the UK, by Sunday Times in 2008.

Within 13 years, she amassed a fortune of more than 700 million US dollars.

Not bad for a writer that 'should go back to school for learning English'. Not bad for somebody that bit the establishment in the back and created her own unique Art in Words. What better motivation for writing in your own unique artistic style.

Writing Outlines.

The Five Elements of a good story: Character, Setting, Plot, Conflict, Resolution.

Ok, then set out, describe your character, let him do a few dances and sing some songs. Two pages before they are boring. *Then we create a setting,* it is dark night when she is walking home. The streets are empty – five pages before it become overdone. *Throw in a twist,* somebody peeking through the foliage in the park; see her walking … add two pages. *Conflict is coming to the pages.* The peeping tom jumps from the bush, grabs the girl around the throat and pulls her into the park. Get to a bench and do what he think he want to do. *Just for the measure,* we bring in a passer-by that hears her screaming. Run up; confront the peeper, the peeper run away. Ahh, now we added five pages. *Then the final resolution* – they drink tea at her apartment and lived happily ever after. There done. *Story reached 20-pages. Where in the hell is my 200-page target?*

Basic Structure of any book.

It does not matter whether you are writing a five hundred-page novel or single page article. There are always three sections. Introduction, Body, Conclusion – in that order. Maybe your 'body' can be in two or three parts. That is easy, yet – it is only a fundamental basic law. There is not much help from staring at those three words to define your story.

Here are some other plots or outlines. I rephrased them according to keywords or actions rather than 'scientific' names. This is only to get an overview of what a typical basic structure is about, I will refer back to these on a later stage.

Outline 1: Anticipation, Call to Action, Frustration, Chaos, Action/Reaction, and Redemption.

Outline 2: Opportunity, New Situation, Change of plans, Progress, Point of no Return, Complications, Higher stakes, Major Setback, Final push, Climax.

Outline 3: Trigger event, Set the stage, Problems, Turning point, Partial Recover from problem, Reawaken the Problem with complications, resolve the problem, resolution.

Outline 4: Inciting an incident, setup scene, complications, turn away, crisis, climax, catastrophe.

Funny thing is that when I sat down and wrote a short summary about my Big Story in these outlines, I ended up with an outline of one page – and a story of ten pages. Then I found myself staring at that abyss again. *"What else could I do to make more pages?"* Then I expanded a bit with the Six-Plot outline.

The 'Six Plot Structure'.

This gives six outline sections for your book with a transition between each (in brackets). Setup (Opportunity) New Situation (Change of Plans) Progress (Point of no Return) Complications (Major Setback) Final push (Climax) Aftermath.

Set-Up.

This is an expansion of the Introduction. Here you introduce the starting scene or environment of your story as well as your main characters. Maybe add in an incident that will be the basis of your story. That leads to the Opportunity for your characters to do something.

New Situation.

Before very much can happen, you bring in a new development. This is the unexpected action point, the suspense. Something threatens the main character, his life, his believes, his personality. It forces him to Change his Plans. Maybe to do or consider options he did not want to do.

Progress.

By now, things are going well. The main character is getting the problems sorted out, the story relaxes a little, but that is just a breath long. Let some incidents push your hero in a direction he does not really want to go. Moreover, beyond the Point of no Return. Now he is locked in for the rollercoaster ride – no getting out before the end of the ride.

Complications.

Just when everybody thinks Peace on Earth, the golden beach under a palm tree with margarita is on the way – break all the nice plans, destroy the progress. From the unexpected side-line, a disaster breaks it all apart. Things never go wrong on only one front. Remember the magical three? Why not let three things go wrong all at once? Major Setback in all the nice plans. Car breaks down, girlfriend abducted, while trying to walk back to town the hero stumbles and strains his ankle. Hammer the hero, make the reader feel so sorry for the poor man (or woman).

Final push.

All bets on the table. It is either going to be a victory or destruction. Depends whom you want to destroy. This is the last fight, the struggle to win her heart or lose all. You are building the tension until the final climax. Climax. Exhausted the fall back on the bed, panting breathless.

Aftermath.

The hero reports to his commander. "I am going to an island for a bit of R&R. See you later". How about *"He got on his horse and ride off into the sunset."* That was the last time anybody saw him. Or the lovely, most famous – with an added tail. "They happily lived ever after with many kids". Maybe you are writing a sequel, then the villain open his eyes in hospital and whispered, "I am going to make that bastard suffer".

Things are looking better. Now we have six sections to write about, let us say 1,500 words on each plus five transitions of maybe 500 words. At least we are getting to pass the 11,000-word count – but that is still a mere 25 pages. I am still going to have a long drawn out struggle to get my 200-page book.

As we go on in this book, you will learn more and more about structures for writing. Let us take a short look at the typical movie structure. After all, we all love a good movie!

Basic Movie structure:

Act 1 – Teaser, characters, intensification, middle acts, conflict.

Act 2 – Assessment (Act on Conflict), Middle Act, Crisis.

Act 3 – Reassessment on Crisis, Main act, Perpetua (defeat but reveal key to possible solution).

Act 4 – Reassessment according to new information, Climax, Denouement – Reviews experience.

Maybe all or any of the above would be sufficient. As for me – they were absolute no help in designing a story that will reach anything more than maybe twenty pages! I found the movie script writing based on the Blake Snyder Beat Sheet. That was a major breakthrough in my writing. It helped me to reach easily to 50 or even 70 pages.

The Blake Snyder Beat Sheet.

A beat-sheet is a film script term, indicative of the smallest single piece of activity in a movie. It could be something the actor does or says or do while he says, even just a pause in action or dialogue. A series of beats makes for a larger Scene (or clip). A number of Scenes builds an Act. As example "John pour coffee into his beaker. Turned around and sat down at the table. He opened his notebook and start typing." These are four beats. Here is another three beats 'As Sandra walk up the stairs. She replies, "*I am sick and tired of your nagging. Please leave me alone.*' Her hand quiver on the cool handrail.'

In novel writing, we will mostly use a number of beats in a paragraph. The paragraph is a scene, and a number of paragraphs (scenes) will form an Act. The Act is our chapter. If you apply this structure in your book, it will not only make for easy reading – but it will make more relevant writing. However, there is a small picture and a larger one. The whole book could be in three or four Acts, each Act can consist of a number of Scenes (Chapters).

From this concept of beats in script writing, comes the 'Beat Sheet'. The Beat Sheet is a basic outline of your book, divided in Acts with Scenes. Each of these no more than a single line description. Although it is called a Beat Sheet, it does not really contain 'Beat' details. To illustrate, here is a short Beat Sheet;

Introduction – In the desert of North Africa. Man struggle to survive.

Characters – Back flash: Johnny and Sarah argument. J kills S by accident. He runs away. Aircraft accident in desert.

Intensification – J arrives in town. Military arrest. Escape.

Middle acts – Steal boat. Run out of fuel in middle of sea. Life threatening situation.

Conflict – J is rescued by human traffickers . . .

Climax – Extradition. Short Court case. Sentence.

Conclusion – J walking into cell at prison.

I learned about the "Story Outline" and I tried a few of them. However, every one of them seems to lack something. The one 'outline system' which I found the closest to perfect was the above Hollywood – Blake Snyder Beat Sheet. It is a great outline – but it is the same frame used for nearly all movies and so many books. That is why you know, at the beginning of the book (or movie), how the whole book will flow and end. Boring, yes, then one have ask if this is still working money wise, do I really need to re-invent the wheel?

You do need to make an outline. That is the unfortunate fact. Without an outline, your great book will end after the first few pages. I can really attest to this. There is none less than fourteen incomplete action thrillers on my computer. One barely came past the description of my famous to be main character. The Blake Beat Sheet helped me a lot. I got my books in no time up to forty or even seventy pages.

Let us first look at the Blake Sheet. Remember, this system is meant for script writing, movies, but it is adoptable to book writing. When you look through this bullet points you will see the exact way nearly all Hollywood movies are structured. It is a good outline for books, but I will show you a better one later. A 'beat' is an individual piece of action in a movie – or in your book. See it as the individual bricks in building a house, palace or shopping complex. *(I copied this 'as-is' from various sources.)*

ACT ONE: (Introduction).

Opening Scene.

Present the struggle and tone of the story. Very much like a news article, a quick outline of what the story will be like. The main character's problem, before the adventure begins.

Set-up.

Expand on the opening scene, present the main character's world as it is, and what is missing in their life. Define the environment and of location of your story.

State the Theme.

What your story is about; the message, the truth. Usually, it is spoken to the main character or in their presence, but they do not understand the truth...not until they have some personal experience and context to support it.

Catalyst.

The moment where life changes. It is the command, telegram, the act of catching her loved-one cheating, allowing a monster on board the ship, meeting the true love of his life, etc.

Debate.

Change is scary and for a moment, or a brief number of moments, the main character doubts the journey they must take. Can I face this challenge? Do I have what it takes? Should I go at all? It is the last chance for the hero to chicken out.

ACT TWO: (Main Body).

The main character makes a choice and the journey begins. We leave the "Thesis" world and enter the upside-down, opposite world of Act One.

B Story – This is when there's a discussion about the Theme – the nugget of truth. Usually, this discussion is between the main character and the love interest. So, the B Story is often called the "love story".

The Promise of the Premise – This is the fun part of the story. This is when Henry's relationship with Sandra blooms, when Indiana Jones tries to beat the Nazis to the Lost Ark, when the detective finds the most clues and dodges the most bullets. This is when the main character explores the new world and the audience is entertained by the premise they have been promised.

Midpoint – Dependent upon the story, this moment is when everything is "great" or everything is "awful". The main character either gets everything they think they want ("great") or does not get what they think they want at all ("awful"). Not everything we think we want is what we actually need in the end.

Bad Guys Close In – Doubt, jealousy, fear, foes both physical and emotional regroup to defeat the main character's goal, and the main character's "great / awful" situation disintegrates.

All is Lost – The opposite moment from the Midpoint: "awful / great". The moment that the main character realizes they have lost everything, they gained, or everything they now have has no meaning. The initial goal now looks even more impossible than before. Something or someone dies. It can be physical or emotional, but the death of something old makes way for something new to be born.

Dark Night of the Soul – The main character hits bottom, and wallows in hopelessness. The "Why hast thou forsaken me, Lord?" Mourning the loss of what has "died" – the dream, the goal, the mentor character, the love of your life, etc. You must fall completely before you can pick yourself back up and try again.

ACT THREE: (Conclusion).

Thanks to a fresh idea, new inspiration, or last-minute Thematic advice from the B Story (usually the love interest), the main character chooses to try again.

Finale – This time around, the main character incorporates the Theme – the nugget of truth that now makes sense to them – into their fight for the goal because they have experience from the A Story and context from the B Story. Act Three is about Synthesis!

Final Image – opposite of Opening Image, proving, visually, that a change has occurred within the character or environment.

Here is a nice sample listing of more than 110 outlines based on the Blake Snyder Beat Sheet.

http://www.savethecat.com/beat-sheets-alpha

In my humble opinion.

The Blake Snyder sheet is only rolling in one way; it does not allow for too many variations. Definitely, it does not help you with options when you stuck on the edge of the abyss. I find this above system good, but not perfect for my personal book writing purpose.

It did not took a long time before I realized that the perfect outline is in our own human anatomy. Actually, we can look at the formation of our being and from there we can learn how to write a great outline. With the following outline, you can easily get more than 33 unique parts in your book, each with hundreds of variations. If you write an average of 1,000 words for each chapter, you have the perfect short book of 50 pages or a nice medium size novel of 200 pages with 4,000 words per section.

Spinal Anatomy.

Before I go on to explain my Spinal Structure for a book, allow me to take you on a short detour into the wonders of the human body.

Right in the beginning of your existence, two opposites came together. It was an ovum from your mother (Female) and a sperm from your father (Male). Guess what – you have the perfect base for a story! The coming together of two opposing forces, right there you have the amount of options your book can form into – more than 300 million sperms fights to claim the only ovum. Which one is going to form your main character? That is how many stories you can start to write. Following the sperm actions, they fight, they die, they wait and eventually maybe 200 will be strong enough to reach the Palace of Creation. Only one, seldom any more, will be able to claim the trophy – to become your protagonist. Maybe two reach the same ovum – twins. The one is the Protagonist the other Antagonist.

The very first part of the human that develop from that union is the Medulla Oblongata. That is the central control station for the whole human being. From here, the signals will go out to develop and control all of the functions of the human from the first week after the opposites come together, until the day the human passes his / her last breath. This is a knob on top of the spinal cord; it links the body to the brain.

The next development is the spinal cord, followed by the brain – both linked through the Medulla Oblongata. At about 4 weeks, the main nervous systems develops, these are now within a 'sack', which will eventually become the skin of the baby. The nervous system starts the development of the various organs –

all controlled from the Medulla Oblongata. There is the heart, the eyes, ears, mouth, stomach, pancreas . . .

The very first hard parts to form are the vertebrae, which are to protect the spinal cord, and the scull, which will protect the brain. There are 33 vertebrae and between each of them, there is a cushion – from where nerves are passing through to the rest of the body. If your spine is perfect and healthy, your body is in good shape.

There are 33 vertebrae divided into five groups.

The Cervical – neck that consist of seven vertebrae.

Then we have the Thoracic – forms your chest cage and it has 12 vertebrae that are linked to 12 pairs of ribs.

Following that are the five Lumbar vertebrae, which is around your tummy, lower torso.

Then five sacral vertebrae – these are the lower back where your hips are about.

Finally the five coccyx; normally some are fused together, almost like one.

Thus in total we have 33 bones (Vertebrae) forming our spinal cord.

The spinal column of bones controls the movement of the body, but its prime function is actually to protect the extension part of your brain, the spinal cord. If the spinal cord is broken, anything lower than that severed location will stop functioning.

The next part of our review is a bit complicated; the body makes some provisions for duplication and redundancy to help the human survive. It is not strictly true that each nerves passing out from each vertebrae only controls one organ, sometimes there are as many as five or six different exiting nerves all going to the same organ. In the anatomy, this is becoming a bit complicated. Below is an interesting image showing more or less, how the various organs are connected to the brain. Do take note of how the organs proceed in order from top down. That is the basic outlay for a perfect book framework.

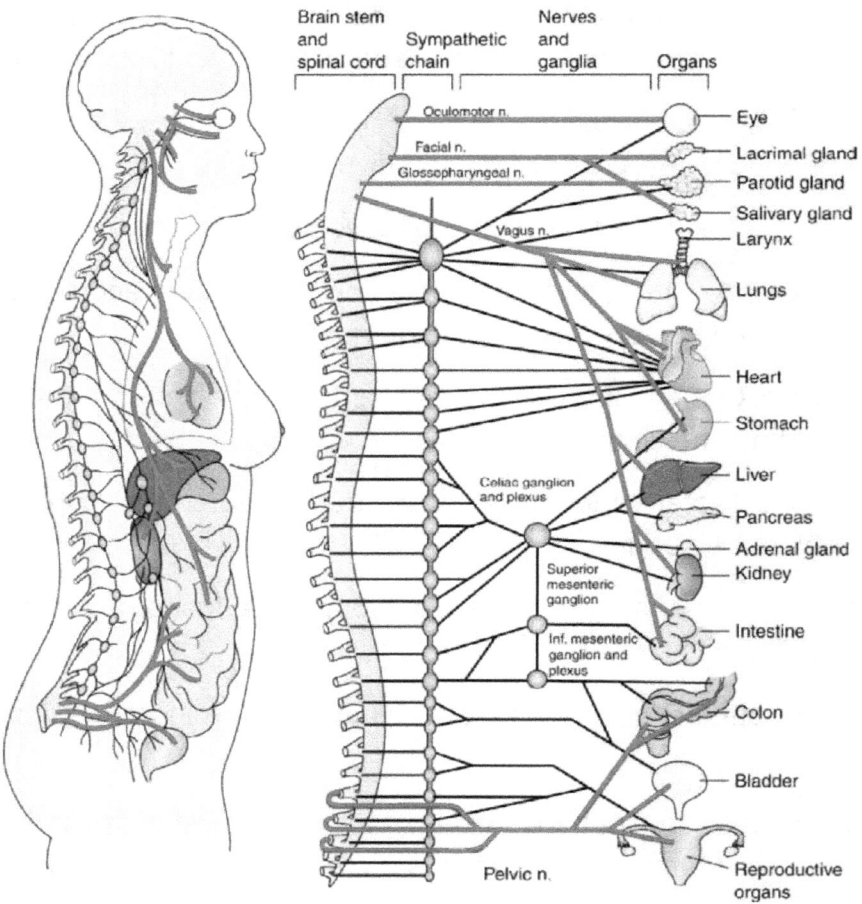

The Eye can see, it observes and it is sensitive. Use this as an introduction to your book; the overview or as prologue leading into your main story. Also, keep this as one critically important target for your writing. Do not tell your story – Show the reader. Let the reader experience rather than read. The mouth, which tells, and dialogue is much lower than the eye – in writing that is of lesser importance.

Lacrimal Gland – these two glands are the tear glands. This is where you catch the reader. Something happens, tears are flowing – be it emotional, hurting, or just a strong wind. This is the point where you set your book in motion.

Parotid Glands – another pair of glands, in this case they are the saliva excreting. Without the saliva, your food will not digest well. These glands are inside the mouth at the back of your jawbone. Use these to introduce a 'digestion' assistance to the reader. Make them know about something that will happen later. Alternatively, to explain some complicated issue. This is your first step for a page-turner novel.

Salivary Glands – These are in the outer side of your upper teeth and under your tongue. In creatures like snakes and Komodo dragons – these are also the poisonous saliva. Here you can go left – and add more digestion for later incidents; or you can go the right by adding the poison to your story. This is where the murder takes place or where she saw the man of her dreams walking past the window.

Larynx – That is the part of your body that makes most of the noise. The larynx creates your voice. Now it is time to define your main character. Alternatively, you can bring in either a romantic opening, or the scream of somebody in pain, somebody discovers a body – or the soldier shouting warnings to his mates. This is the first Big Bang of your book.

The lungs – Sure, you know what lungs does. They exchange oxygen with carbon dioxide in the blood. The blood is flowing throughout the whole body. Sufficient oxygen and the body functions well. Lack of oxygen and there are problems in the body. The lungs are linked to the nose, which smells. Use the nose to bring in the next page-turner in your story. Add more feeling, or deepens the plot; use the lungs to fill the intrigue of your storyline. There are two lungs; maybe you can have a split in your story line? The lungs also supplies the air through the larynx that makes noise – or talking. Ahh, but inhaling poisonous gas, to the lungs, might kill or incapacitate your characters. What about clearing out the lungs, phlegm, smoking . . . ?

Do remember – there are plenty of options, with each organ, to twist your story!

The Heart – Well, this is the pumping station of your whole body. It is the energy. Now you need to pulse the flow of the story up. Action, flushing feelings of anticipation. This is the tension, the higher you can get the blood pressure, the more things can happen. Do not forget the heart has four chambers and it pumps blood to the brain as well as everywhere else in the body. The heart is also a symbol of emotion – be it love, compassion, anger or something dark and sinister. The heart can suffer unexpected failure – heart attack. It has to be protected at all times, all the blood passes through the heart. Is the heart of your story about love, or hate, or revenge?

The Stomach – Time to feed your story with something unexpected. It can be food, spicy, soft, and creamy or gut wrenching poison. In truth, this is where the main part of your story plays off. No food is no life. It is the last and final passage to lock your reader in, forever, to the end of this book and right on into your next book. Remember the word 'gut feeling'.

The Liver – The liver has many important functions. It helps with digestion by producing bitter bile for the stomach, it detoxify and cleans the blood flowing to the brain, generates the heat in your body. Did you know the liver is the largest gland in your body? So what is a gland? Glands produce various chemical substances that are required by other organs in the body. Another main part for your book. Let the liver make the healing substance for all the stress. Bring the story a little back to balance, let the stress cool down a bit. Or, lit the fireworks. What will happen if the liver makes the wrong chemicals? What if it fails completely, or overheats. The options are phenomenal.

The Pancreas – Oh, how we love sweetness. Love is in the air. Everything calms down. Well, maybe not. What if the pancreas is not controlling the sugar in the blood? What if the sweet sugar is too much, or too little? Can we get to the insulin in time? Is there a total breakdown – or do you give the story a little pause with a nice sweet ice cream?

The Adrenals – Jump! These two little attachments to your kidneys are the Fight or Flight boosters. That tingling feeling you get the second before you jump from a fright. Ah, there is a big monster breaking the window. All just when you thought everything is fine, under control by the pancreas. Now this happens. Time for a severe fight scene – or fleeing the scene. Maybe the girl is very unhappy with her boyfriend, now she locks herself away in a treehouse. The International Space Station is crashing on the Earth. Whatever you do – it has to be filled with adrenaline. Fast, serious, big-bang.

The Kidneys – They clean toxins and minerals from the blood. They also control blood viscosity. How well the blood will flow through the body depends on the function of the kidneys. If they are in good working order, everything is fine. However, if there are problems, things can go really wrong. There is no pain on earth that beats that of a big kidney stone. There is not much that can be done about that, either. A sudden sheering pain come into your story, or maybe it is the aftermath of your lovely couple laying in sweat on the bed after fire filled sex.

Intestines – This is the long running tube from your stomach. It is where the body absorbs its nutrients from, together with healing medicine – or bad poison. Things go a little slow, but whatever the body absorbs here is going to formulate the next part of your book – or maybe the next book. The intestines has three sections; duodenum, jejunum, and ileum. In particular, you can have an appendix that burst, severe pain, deadly potential. Most stomach ulcers and cancers are actually in the Duodenum and not really in the stomach itself. You have amazing potential to expand your story here.

The Colon – This is where the body absorbs fluids and process the material that needs to be disposed from the body. The end of the Colon is the rectum from where you drop the smelly ones. There are four parts – Ascending colon, Transverse colon, Descending colon and Sigmoid colon. This is where you start to wind your story down. The good (or evil) rules. If you plan on a series of books, which I really recommend . . . do remember that the waste feces you are dropping; that is good food for a new cycle of life – food for insects and fertilizer for plants. Start to run-in for your next book. In your story, this is where the hero and his maiden are sitting exhausted under the tree next to the ravine.

The Bladder – Another disposal system from the body. Urine is acidic; it serves no purpose for life. Needs to just clean out. End your book. Or …

Reproductive System – Let the story go on and have the wildest erotica you can imagine. This is also, where you plant the seed for the sequel in your story. Let it all begin over again. Remember the villain that everyone thought was dead, but . . .

Do keep this one important issue in mind. You do not have to use all of the above. You can even just use the five main groups of vertebrae – the neck, chest, stomach, pelvic and coccyx. If you plan on a big book, why not expand? These organs above are just the main ones, and their functions I described is also just some of what they actually do.

Get hold of an anatomy book – or use the internet – and collect more information about all of these organs and the others. They all can work together in various combinations to be the spine of a few thousand books. How many diseases are there? Each could be a different path in your book about erotica, or action thriller, or sci-fi creation.

We did not even reach to the point of body parts! Remember there is the head, the ears, the arms, elbows, wrists, hands, fingers; legs … all can be used in a place, from the spine – to enhance your story plot.

Practical Application.

For the sake of argument, you design a short story with only five parts – based on the main sections of the spine. The genre is a romantic novel. Now you are making the outline and see how your story will flow. Then you start writing. Somewhere in the second part, you suddenly find yourself in a cul-de-sac.

What 'organ' were you writing about? The Heart, ok let us see what can we throw in. How about the girlfriend's father had a sudden heart attack? Now she needs the protagonist's help. There your story goes on track again.

Are you stuck somewhere in the Main Body? You cannot imagine where you can add into the storyline, you need some action. Can we use the kidney? How about a sudden sheering pain of a kidney stone?

The protagonist is shot by accident, just because he was in the wrong place at the wrong time. He is sitting in a restaurant on the esplanade, drinking a cold beer and pondering all the things that happened earlier. A sudden noise, car driving down the road. Sounds like fireworks. He feels a tug at his shoulder. See his shirt turning red, what happened? Why is he feeling so dizzy? When he woke up in hospital, they told him that he was shot; by a terrorist driving down the road and randomly shooting at people.

A sudden, unexpected, realistic incident. Many following options on letting the story flow.

Base your story outline on the human anatomy, structured according to the spine. Whenever you are stuck in writing, or ideas running out, grab an Anatomy book. See what organs or glands, diseases or properties are in that region – and how enzymes, minerals, elements or activity can affect those. Then look at that component and consider how you can twist that into your story.

The Spine of your Book.

Before you even start writing your story, you MUST outline the story. If you create a good successful outline, then your story is going to flow, from start to finish in a very short time, effectively. Fail to have a good outline is (probably) guaranteed failure of your dream story.

Throughout the next part I am going to refer to the Spinal Anatomy, we introduced in the previous chapter. Once you understand these basics, you will be amazed to see how any book you wish to write – will just flow out. Remember the very first part that formed as a new human? The Medulla Oblongata, that knob on top of your spine. The control centre of your complete physical being, connecting the brain to the body. Well, that is also true in your book writing.

Medulla Oblongata = Premise Line of your book.

The Premise line is the most important part of your book. It is also the shortest. You must be able to define your whole book in a well-constructed pitch line. Typically, do not use more than 50 words. You know the famous six magical words for any problem - Who, What, When, Why, Where and How. The Premise line must define three of these questions while leaving the rest in suspense. Two of the 'W' is Must-Have – the What and Who of your story.

Spinal Cord = Protagonist of your story.

The next step in the Anatomy development is the Spinal cord. For our book – that is the Main Character. Everything else will be around this main character, but it does not end there. As the spinal cord links the whole body together – and to the brain; your main character is the link between your story and the reader. The protagonist has to feed the reader with nutrients, information and energy; while the reader guides your storyline. Well, sort of, in the way that you have to write the story the reader wants to read! Without a good healthy spinal cord, the body will suffer and the brain will feel the pain, or lack of any feeling. Do not let this happens to your reader with a lack of character in your protagonist.

Bone Marrow = The Antagonist of your story.

This is a VERY important character. The villain, the bad boy, the opposition; or the one that will change. Besides, for this character being the bad boy, the Antagonist is the motor that drives your story. If there is no bone marrow, there will be no blood. The book will not survive beyond the first page. In truth, I think the Antagonist is more important than the Protagonist is. Where your main character is Omni present from the spinal cord; the Antagonist is everywhere, but not centre stage all the time.

The Brain = The Reader.

After the development of the spinal cord, the next part of the human body to develop is the brain. In our analogy the brain is the reader of our story, we are going to ignore that for the rest of this book structure. Only keep in mind that the spinal cord feeds the brain, and the brain dictates the signals to the rest of the body. Thus, your protagonist is the intermediary between your book and the reader. Write your book for the reader to experience all six senses of the body - through the Main Character.

Vertebrae = Desire of your main character.

Every human being has three main desires; Survival, Security, Society in that order. The vertebrae that protect the spinal cord represent these. It is protection for the spinal cord, allows flexibility and strength. There are 33 bones; each can play a related role in the society of your main character. Between each bone is a linking soft bone – the disk. If that is pressed or damaged, it causes great pain; which acts as a shock on the brain. Keep this in mind for conflict and surprises.

While we are looking at the complete column, we also noticed there are five sections. The neck – which allows the head to turn and the senses in the head to focus on a particular issue. The thoracic that keeps on working without being noticed – heart, lungs, liver, etc. The stomach region that acts digests and feeds in the background and the lower spine, which is either in resting or active motion. See how you can spin your story around the human anatomy?

Rib Cage = Comfort, safety and protection.

The most critical organs of your body are protected in the rib cage; the heart, lungs, and the liver. Without these organs, you will not survive more than four minutes. Further, the nerves that works with these organs comes from different vertebrae. In writing your story, you can change the sequence of these organs around, as you wish. Be it first a cleaning, then pumping then adding fuel and pumping again – or first the love affair then add heating the scene up and add more erotica until finally get to think clearly again.

The Lower Torso = Vulnerability.

The lower half of the body is less protected than the upper half. Here is where your main character will experience his biggest attack. It is time to let the adrenaline out, to fight for life or death. This is where all the food that that you set on the table, is to be digested. There is no perfect order in which you can play the scenes here. Adrenaline, gut feelings, fighting disease, absorbing knowledge, disposing of dead bodies … there are so many action, conflict and options it is beyond believe.

Pelvic Region = Final climax or Recreation.

We all love this region. Hmm that tight round ass, the soft lips of kissing, portals to the fragrant garden … Here you can play the climax of the love scene. Here you can also start the war. The sperm has to come from somewhere. Again, one can play with the framework of your book, so many options. Do remember the rectum is part of this section, so are the hips, legs and feet. Do not forget the knees; maybe in desperation a prayer is needed? A priest comes around for guidance. On the other hand, on your knees it is easy for ISIS to chop your head off.

Oxygen, Nutrients = Incidents.

Like the main character, all the incidents must relate to the overall body of your book. In the same, there is also a true point to remember. Do not keep on referring back to old history in too many snips, for too long time. Just like your body will not survive on poor oxygen or old nutrients.

Enzymes and hormones = Controls of the body.

Use the concepts of enzymes and hormones, as in the physical anatomy, to control your story line. Like a large complicated network of delicate links that runs from the pancreas to the kidney and from the Thyroid to the duodenum. These give you perfect opportunity to bond your whole story into a singularity. However, do not try to write ten short stories in one book!

Others.

Keep in mind this is a very superficial outline of possibilities. I did not even touch on the energy flows in the body, or lymph, the difference between veins and arteries … Do not forget the bacteria and viruses.

Here is a portion sample of the Beat Sheet draft for my book "Expansion". Notice how I use a photo in place of text; it generates a lot of ideas and words.

Working Title:	Expansion						
Start construction	15-Aug-16						
Author:	Corrie Lamprecht						
Presmise:	A space capsule lands on the moon. Two astronaughts. Drilling samples. Cave in. Underground chamber. Stange objects. Explore. Not cave but space ship. Human skeletons. Unknown writings. Find hieroglyphic crystal. No radio contact. Time elapse. Get out - 4 years passed, for them only 2 hours. They are not alone anymore.						
Main Character:	Comander Timothy G. Foster	Tim		Secondary Character:	Lt. Herbert G. Mallory		HG
Main Opponent:				Secondary Opponent:			
Message Target							

Size = 1,500 words				Neck			Stock Icons
Notes	Icon	Characters	Keywords	Story Image & Ideas	Other Considerations		
Prologue			Lander pod leave from ship. Argument				
Set the Scene			Moon landscape. Near Dark. 2019.				
Introduction			Space exploration from earth has gone viral. Why?				
Transition			Door opening, stepping out, Dust.				

Size =		Chest (Rib Cage)		Story split in two time frames - two			Stock Icons
Notes	Icon	Main Characters	Keywords	Time inside Object - slowing	Real Time - Mothership.		
			Magnetic anomaly. Take lander transsport - like quad		Normal routines in Mothership. Maintenance, repairs, reports.		
			Collecting Samples. Out of range from Earth coms for next	Tim think of his daughter, now 12 years old. She wants to follow his footsteps into space travel.	Contaot lost with Team 2. Send Rescue Team #1. Find no traces of Team 2. But find the mineral		
			Split Story. On moon the two astraonaughts	Collecting mineral samples. One such was red salty like in a large lake deposit - Promethium	Outside world: Declare them missing. Big Mystery. Follow up team find rock samples. Have		
				HG is thinking about his commander. On college they were good friends. It should be him that	Tim's Daugher on land. Miss father. Memorial services. Go on. Determined to become		
				They find holographic crystal. No signs of occupants. Strange kind sof instruments.	Interested in Biology, Genetics.		

If you are interested in my free blank MS-Excel 2013 Beat Sheet and Character Profile, please e-mail me at

corrielamprecht@outlook.com

You do not have to use this Excel sheet. You can use Google Docs to create your Beat Sheet; or you can even use physical storyboard like the image below with sets of cards or sticky notes.

A great idea is often to use photos, images or hand drawings in place of notes on your storyboard.

Below is one of J.K. Rowling Plot outlines.

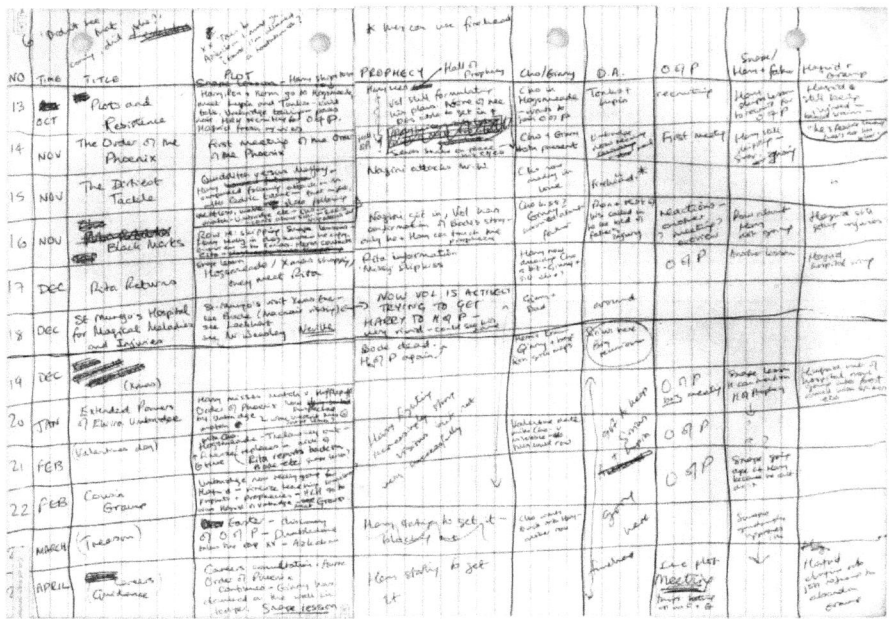

This one here is a physical Storyboard from Fiona Harper with sticky notes that are easy to shift around, insert or remove another.

The Elements.

Writing a successful book is by no means an exact science. Just as no two human beings are 100% the same. Just look at their DNA, fingerprints, or blood samples. So is it with writing stories. Some people say there are three elements, other say there are five or seven, or thirty. This just shows how diverse the possibilities are.

However many there are, it is irrelevant. What is true is that some elements are of critical importance. These elements could be the main sections of your book – or it could be the smaller scenes or even in a series of beats. Throughout your story, the elements are the blood of your story. It carries oxygen, nutrients, and hormones and keeps everything in the body operational. It also distributes bacteria and viruses!

Here is quite a comprehensive list of 'Elements for Writing'. It is a good practice if you can include all in your book, but that is quite unlikely. Whichever you like – and will fit in with your writing style – use them. Move the other elements to the back of your mind for the 'in-case-and-maybe'.

There are two groups of elements: The Must Have and the Optional.

The Must Have Elements.

This group of elements must be like a string, right through your book from start to finish. You can twist and turn them, you can change them as much as you like, but they are of critical importance.

The Genre (Category).

Although it is not part of your writing, it is everything of your book. Never jump in and start writing your story. Each type of genre (category) book has its own suitable style. If you write a lovely romantic story, but use Sci-Fi style – the book will fail. Same if you are using a long detailed romantic writing style in a War Thriller – it will not work. People pick their books according to the genre they are interested in. I am not one for reading love stories and my girlfriend will never read a Horror story.

The Premise Line.

Once you decided on the Genre, you need to describe your story in less than 50 words. This should be your focus for the whole book. Print it out on paper and stick it on your computer screen where you can see it every few seconds. Do not lose that main thread until your first draft is finished. You can edit your premise while writing. This would also be the selling point of your book, your pitching line to the potential buyer.

The Opposing Characters.

Off course, there must be a main character. This element has to be defined as early as possible; Page 1 is the best location. Following that, you should not hang around too long before you introduce the main opponent. Say within the first 10% of your book. There are many variations. As example, the opposing character can be the same as the main character – but a psychological tug-of-war going on within that person about a particular issue.

Scene Setting.

Although the introduction of the two main opponents is part of the scene setting, it is also important to tell the reader in what environment the story is starting. Time-period, environment, location, etc. This is where the option of 'Show' is often more applicable – but not always. Your scene setting might include a description of the bedroom where the murder took place, or the desert sands and dunes where the shipwreck lies on the beach.

Your scene setting could be a detailed setting, but it might not always be the best option. It could be a simple two short lines *"Day 5 - 02h34 – On the ship Odessa somewhere in the Caspian Sea"*. Now here you clearly get a gut feeling. Suspense. Something is going to happen. Just the simple line will make the readers mind race ahead. What is going to happen? Why is this on a ship? Why in the Caspian Sea? Why such odd hours?

Guess why this powerful short statement is so effective? Your reader immediately wants to have answers. They will start turning the pages.

Scene setting can be once for the whole book, or at the beginning of every chapter. Do not make two scenes in the same chapter.

By having a more descriptive scene setting, your story line is flowing slower. On the other hand, it gives a deeper insight and allows for more emotion. Very nice for romantic or erotic type of writing. For action – better to let as much as possible to the imagination of the reader. Single words like Desert, open Ocean, Top of Cliff …

Action.

Drop those long TV Soapy dialogues. Well, unless you are writing a TV soapy. That is the most boring books to read. Create action. Your characters, scenes, and story – they all must contribute to action. I don't only mean action like Terminator shooting Alien. Action is also when the boy grabs hold of the girl's ponytails. The car failed to stop at the traffic light. No action = no page turning.

Conflict.

This is always an important element. Be it the conflict between Superman and Batman – or between the wife and girlfriend of a confused man. It does not need to be conflict between two people; a very good form of conflict is the inner arguments. When the protagonist is forced to do something against his will. The inner arguments of a doctor who needs to pull the plug on an ICU patient. The married man that fight with his inner emotions when a pretty girl offers him a magnificent view of certain body parts. The conflict between France and Germany in WWII. The more conflict you can create throughout your novel, the more interesting the reader will be. However – it MUST be relevant to your story, it must reflect your Premise line. Important, all conflict must be resolved by the end of your story, even if it is only a book or two later.

Clarity and Simplicity.

This is my own addition. If you are writing poetry or a work of literature – then this is not valid. If you are writing a book for leisure reading – then, please, do use simple easy everyday words rather than complicated strings of mathematical like arguments. Do not make your reader seeking the help of a thesaurus on every page, best if not ever during the whole book. Use shorter sentences. Not only do the long sentences slow the story flow down, it also requires more difficult structuring and sometimes complicated words. Use simple straight forward, clear words and ideas. This is one such horrible example not to use in a leisure book: *"From brocade is become to bold a thief, as we, the robed leauerage, and pittie it. The fluggith gaping auditor deuoures; he merkes not whole, it was . . . "* Hmm, I am still trying to decipher that piece of English Literature, even with Google. For such work, you might get praise from my friend Harry, but then Harry loves anything that he cannot understand.

Writing an enjoyable novel is about the story; not the literacy accomplishments. Transport the reader into a different world; take them out from their 'Now".

The Optional Elements = Writing Style.

The optional elements are good, sometimes important for writing. They are not critical for the book or story itself. I would rather say these are very important for yourself – to develop your Writing Style. You, and only you yourself, can develop these into your own personal style. When you start building a following of readers, they will look for your particular style in writing. Not every writer is the same and definitely not every reader likes the same writing style.

Exaggerate Tales, somewhat.

Use sub-stories, tales, and fables. They are usually welcome – provided it is applicable to the story. Sometimes it is more interesting to tell something as a parable rather than straight out – and visa versa. "He slowly enters her through the Pearly Gate" sounds a bit more romantic than "He entered her". How about; "He entered the collapsed building, found her under some rubble. With brute force he lifted the beam from her crushed leg" – even though a building beam that crushed her leg probably weighs more than a ton. Did you ever notice in movies how the hero's gun never runs out of bullets? When he is alone in a shooting fight with 10 bandits, they always miss him – and every bullet from his gun hits a target? Hmm. Maybe that is a bit overdone. Would it not be better to have a bullet splinter the hero's leg – more conflict, and more drama to write?

Imagination.

Use your imagination while writing, after all any book is about imagination, especially fiction. However, do not deplete all the imagination. You have to tickle the imagination of your reader too. The more you can leave imagination, doubt, questions, etc. in the mind of your reader, the better your story will sell. There is a nice scientific reason. The mind can process hundreds of inputs per second; your written words can only give less than four inputs. The more you guide the imagination, but not give full answer, the better the readers mind is occupied with your story and options in it. If you can succeed in keeping the imagination of the readers mind occupied, in the direction you guide it – the more pages the reader will turn – and the faster they will read. If you can really play this imagination very good in your style, any number of readers will see your story different. Combined with the Tales above, it forms a very strong style of writing. Just look at the Harry Potter series, one of J.K. Rowling most powerful styles – Imagination and Tales.

Irony = Amusement.

A good way to keep the readers mind occupied is using irony. The expression of the words in such way that it actually means the opposite of what is written. Just be careful since irony slows the pace of a story down, on the other hand it can make a good read during a slow period in the story. The nice definition of irony, *"a state of affairs or an event that seems deliberately contrary to what one expects and is often amusing as a result"*.

Humour and Tears.

A good dosage of humour makes the story glow. If you can play on the reader's emotions, draw the tears and make them laugh in the same chapter – then you are a top rate writer. Always create some comical scene, even in serious situations.

Tempo.

There has to be a feeling of slow moving time and times when it seems that time does not exist. In action, go fast tempo, in description, make it slower with more details. However, never make the slow tempo last too long. A golden rule is no more than a thousand words.

Aspiration.

All the time, starting at page one and going to the final climax – there has to be an element of aspiration. A purpose, a target that has to be reached. It is like the breath of your body, all the time, subtle, like a ghost – floating through the words. You should not need to explain this to the reader, it is just 'there' somewhere between the lines. Just like the reader, your story must breathe, sometimes. Building to a climax is better done in step format rather than rocket style.

Tone.

The tone in your story can be scared, anxious, worried, foolish, smart, depressing, joyful, humorous, sad, serious, formal, pessimistic, etc. Although you will develop your own unique style, it is also good to use different tones for different scenes and characters. It is not always, 'what' you say, it is rather 'how' you say it. This technique is about how you string your words and construct your sentences.

Ideal.

Do not write the ideal essay. This is not a college exam. One reason many writers fail is that they all write in classroom style. It does not work in real life. I recently read an Afrikaans book, written completely in Cape Town slang. For me it was very difficult to read, for others it is like music. Regardless, the way the author used the slang words were very compelling; and, they are not in any dictionary and the sentence construction will have any teacher haemorrhaging. Nevertheless, the book sold well, and they made a successful movie about it – "*Chappie (2015)*".

Novelty.

Oh please, do write in your own style. More important than that, write your own story. Do not re-write something everybody watched in the cinema last week. If your book can be completely about something new – then you have a winner. That is what most readers' desire. Hence, romance, Fantasy and Sci-Fi are the biggest genres.

Surprise.

Together with Conflict and Action, surprise is always a great enhancement. It does not have to be a Big Bang, just an unexpected murder, or a sudden kiss from the girl he did not even see coming. Readers will always try to run ahead of your story. It is their normal brain activity. Surprises sort of make up for the slow reading speed. Thus, if you deviate from the expected road – you surprise them. Do make sure your surprise is realistic. Killing the main character and have him magically resurrect a chapter later . . . that, does not go off well.

Questions.

Generate questions in your actual writing is good. A nice technique is to you guide the story in such way that the readers ask the question themselves. Do make sure to answer all the questions that you might have generated, in your words and in your readers mind, eventually. Some can remain, but then make sure the reader knows there is going to be a sequel on your book. It is a very bad feeling to be hanging in suspense. The reader might not buy any other books from you.

Creating Characters.

There are many ways you can create your character – and many books on how to do it. Personally, I am using a very short description, but it gives me pages of understanding and info about my character. Details I can flesh out during the flow of my story – if needed. However, always make sure it does fit the typical personality. The best type of character is the one with whom the reader can associate.

A good character has strong points and has weaknesses; the good and the bad. Combining these two devils in the ear or eye of your character makes for great writing potential. Personally, I like to use the 'Zodiac Moulds'. After all, these are at least 90% true to form in people. More interesting is that you get the perfect basket of personality blends.

Name: You need to know what to call him. Preferably, use 'applicable' names and also call or nick names. To an extend keep practical names. You will for instance not use Sir John Smith as name for a Pigmy in the forest of Congo. Carlos Santorin is quite unlikely to be the President of Russia. It is also silly to use long names, difficult to write and more difficult for the reader. Using for instance "*Wolfeschlegelsteinhausenbergerdorff*" as your protagonist is somewhat stupid, unless . . . Which by the way is a real name and officially the longest name of a person.

Age: Every person changes as they get older. Thus if you need a cheeky little girl character, do not make her a grumpy 64 year old grandmother. Keep the age applicable – and restrictive - in your story. With age comes wisdom and calm. The young are more arrogant risk takers. The grandmother is unlikely to be talking like a 14-year-old girl.

Race: Yes, racism is extremely valid. A Chinese person will see death in a different light than a European or Aborigine in Papua. Make sure you do understand at least a little bit about the culture of your intended character. Typically, one will not use a hot blooded Italian girl as Inuit in Greenland. Well, unless you intend to use that as base for inner conflict.

Zodiac: This is one of my favourite techniques, a great time saver. It is a great advantage since I know both the Chinese and Western zodiacs reasonably well. Thus if I say the person is a Monkey – I have a general personality description stretching over a few pages – in one word. I also know what problems there are in the personality – and use it to present my character throughout the story. In the Chinese system there are 12-animals with five elements; thus you can have a pure blend of 60 character types. Western Zodiac (Month) is another form of character description. Just the word 'Aries' already gives you a good measure of personality. No need to go the Full Monty with detailed star charts here!

In my character sheet, it will be something like Monkey, Ophiuchus, Fire. – hmm, that is me.

Use Google and search for "famous people born as …" From there you can expand and read more about that character, lifestyle – and way of talking. Pick a famous person that is close to your character's requirements. Use that photo on your profile sheet.

Quite interesting is one hidden piece of knowledge. Some more advanced Zodiacs – in particular the Chinese animals – has an interesting bonus. They even describe the physics of your person. So physically, a Monkey will look like this and a Goat will look like that. They will also have basic traits, manners. The Goat often stuff food pieces in their handbag to take home for the kids – or dogs. The Monkey will stand aside for others to scoop the lime light. A Leo person is usually very meticulous and attentive to smallest details.

Demographics: Here I just state the obvious environmental factors that will affect the personality of the character. What was the financial status when growing up, education level, experiences, work CV, what country, city, area did he grew up in, military training, was she the only child . . . All of these little things that contributes to the alteration of a basic Zodiac personality. Always consider the family and friends. Family are not chosen, you get them as parcel deal. A drunken father and shouting pantoffel mother will result in certain character traits in their kids. Then there is the saying "Show me your friends and I tell you who you are". Friends are selected. Thus, the friends of your character will tell you much about the person you are dealing with.

Voice: How will your character speak? What is their typical body posture and body language? Funny how much this will help you in the formation of your story. Usually I either use the personality of somebody I know in real life or one from political, military, movie star, etc. Thus if I base this character on a movie star I may say "Jason Statham – Mechanic". Then I know what kind of personality I have. Using 'Spock' (Star Wars) gives me a nice dry comical yet serious personality that speaks in his own unique way. I might use "Judge Jeanine of Fox" – a very hmm sarcastic, irony type of talking. Alex Jones is a ranting intense character. That way, I will know how to apply my character in his thoughts and dialogue.

Purpose: This is another of my own additions. What is the purpose of this character in my story? Where will he/she enter, in what way and until where is the contribution. In what way will this character contribute to the final resolution of the story?

Some Chinese philosophy. If you know yourself and if you are true to yourself − then you are very fortunate. If you are fortunate, true to form, then you are happy. I have seen so many times, a person that lives a life dictated by society and expectations − in contradiction to what he/she really is . . . such person is always unhappy, grumpy, out of balance and frustrated. You can use this to generate inner conflict. A Tiger that is forced to live as if a Rabbit will be a very unhappy person, and all his action will reflect that.

Question: Do I really need to create a Character sheet in my novel? Well the answer is no, you do not need to. But. If you want to write a good book, you need good realistic characters. The more your reader can associate with your character, the better your story will be. If you do have a well-defined character, then you can concentrate on writing your story. Throw incidents at the character − and use your character sheet to determine what that person would do in such situation.

Using the Chinese system as example: The protagonist is pressed into a corner, a life-threatening situation. If he is a little 'soft fury animal' like a rabbit − he will typically cover down and hope the thread passes, or he will try to outrun the tiger. If on the other hand the protagonist is a Tiger, there will be fur flying. The monkey will use some tool, maybe a crate suspended from a crane cable, or wet floor and electric cable.

If your character is a soft-spoken loving father at home, it is unlikely that he will be a monster at work. Such will confuse your reader and you will lose the bond between the reader and your whole book.

The rest of the page I will leave blank. As I am applying this character, I will keep notes on what traits in their personality I applied. This ensures continuity.

This is my basic MS-Excel Character sheet. Note the 'Comment' applied to some cells, additional space for lots of more detailed information. The photo I used for the character is such that it tells you exactly what kind of personality we are dealing with. The face, beard, worn hat, hairstyle, piercing eyes, background, standing at a gate, gun pointed. It all says rock solid earthy bloke that says *'Don't mess with what is mine'*. The photo and Zodiac signs makes a lot of definition unnecessary. Yet, in any circumstances during my story – I know how the character will react. Consistent. Better still, if your application of the character is good, the reader will soon be able to associate your protagonist with somebody they know and I am sure everybody does know a person like this.

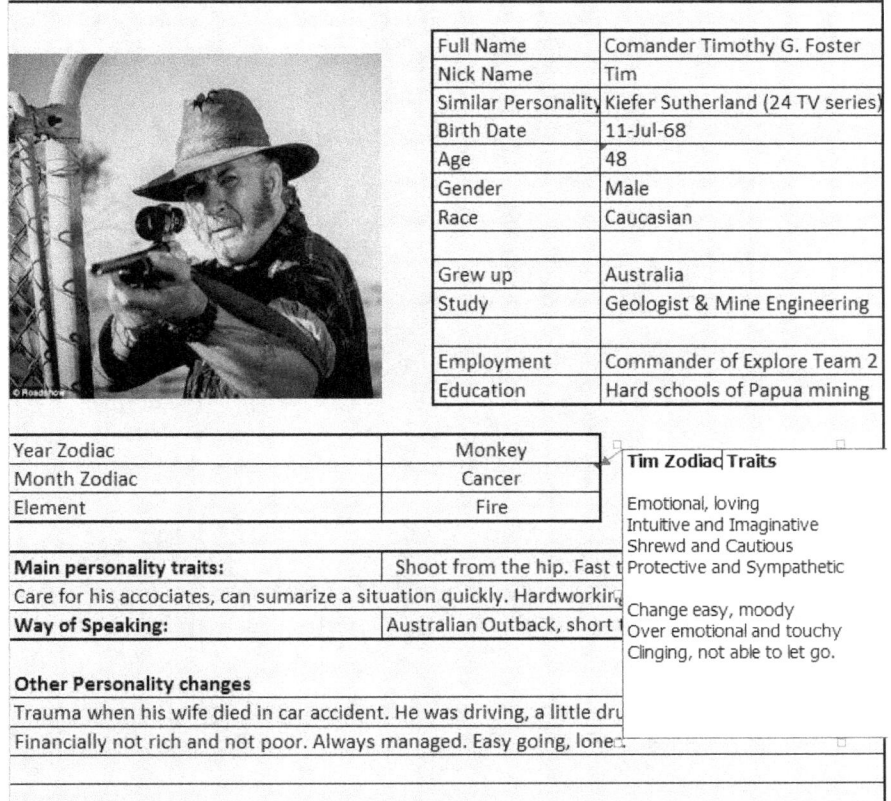

Full Name	Comander Timothy G. Foster
Nick Name	Tim
Similar Personality	Kiefer Sutherland (24 TV series)
Birth Date	11-Jul-68
Age	48
Gender	Male
Race	Caucasian
Grew up	Australia
Study	Geologist & Mine Engineering
Employment	Commander of Explore Team 2
Education	Hard schools of Papua mining

Year Zodiac	Monkey
Month Zodiac	Cancer
Element	Fire

Tim Zodiac Traits

Emotional, loving
Intuitive and Imaginative
Shrewd and Cautious
Protective and Sympathetic

Change easy, moody
Over emotional and touchy
Clinging, not able to let go.

Main personality traits: Shoot from the hip. Fast t
Care for his accociates, can sumarize a situation quickly. Hardworkin
Way of Speaking: Australian Outback, short t

Other Personality changes
Trauma when his wife died in car accident. He was driving, a little dru
Financially not rich and not poor. Always managed. Easy going, lone

PS. Not visible under the comment is a link to a sound clip I took from a movie, speech, or something where the actual voice and speaking style is quite evident. In this case, it is a real outback Australian farmer talking. That helps me to create the voice for this character – and diversify from the other characters I am using in the story.

If you are interested in a free blank MS-Excel 2013 Beat Sheet and Character Profile, please e-mail me at:

corrielamprecht@outlook.com

Dialogue.

There are many courses on dialogue writing, videos and books – even free. Therefore, I am not going to expand much on this. There are only three small issues I would like to point out. For some reason these are not often described in lessons. The dialogue is sometimes the most feared and misused part of a novel book. You can write a whole 100-page novel with as little as 10 beats of dialogue and it will be good. On the other hand, if you write that 100 pages only with dialogue it will be horrible. The golden rule is 'Less dialogue is better'.

However, if you apply the above techniques in your character sheet, and use that as basis of your dialogue, it will be unbeatable. Most important is the issue of Voice as I explained above. Add a sound clip of how you want to imagine the character speaks. Keep geography in mind. A British will for instance say Robot where American will say Traffic Light. Small issues like this makes for an authentic, relatable character.

Keep the dialogue as short as possible and always applicable to the situation and overall story. An Amazon 'Best Seller' I read recently was truly a very good book. It is actually three book series. Overall, it was a Sci-Fi and very well presented action, lots of conflicts and surprises filling more than 600 pages. Around page 450 in the first book, a section stretches over eight chapters with the most drawn out dialogue one can imagine. The worst is that in all three books there is no application of those 28 pages of pointless dialogue. I still do not know why that many wasted pages, but I do know - that section drops my rating of the book from five to four stars.

If you have a scene, especially a dialogue, which could be removed from the book - without affecting the story – then such scene and dialogue should not be in your book. Cut it out.

Keep the actions and dialogue of one character in one paragraph, unless it is very long, then add more paragraphs – no problem there. However, try not have two characters active in the same paragraph. This makes for confusion in the readers mind.

If you change the scene, that is in one paragraph, on its own. Instead of having to say, He said "…" She said"…" he say "…" etc. it is easier to write – and much easier to read and much faster to do different paragraphs. In the following example, it is evident that each paragraph is the other character.

As he is opening the car door for Ann, Mark said, "Let us get into the house quickly".

"But my shoes will get wet."

"It is OK; I have a cloth there on the steps."

"Take my hand; I would not like to fall in this rain."

Mark hold out his arm and guide Ann into the house.

In this example, you wrote fewer words, the reader read faster – and the reader's brain has some additional images to create. Thus, you get a triple win in the short dialogue. That is not all you implanted in the readers brain. Let me just go over the lines again and see if you agree.

As he is opening the car door for Ann, Mark said, "Let us get into the house quickly". Mark is polite and courteous. He cares for Ann. Why do they need to get in the house quickly?

"But my shoes will get wet." Ahh, now we know why they need to get into the house quickly. Readers question answered. Water on the ground, maybe raining? Is Ann a bit selfish? She cares more about her shoes than she does about Mark standing in the rain while holding her door open. She is also conscious

about wet shoes. Is it because she cares about the shoes or is it because she does not want to get wet shoes into the house?

"It is OK; I have a cloth there on the steps." Here we have the gentleman again. There is a cloth. Do not worry. I will take care of your shoes. It also insinuates that Mark is a forward thinking type of man.

"Take my hand; I would not like to fall in the rain." Now we know the answer on the question from line two. Ann is probably a self-centred type person. She is also insecure.

A few months ago, I watched an action movie – one of the "Expendables" series. While writing this I thought about that movie and just watched it again. The whole movie was nearly 140 minutes long. In the entire movie, adding up all the dialogues will be less than ten minutes. Yet, it was quite a successful movie at the box office.

With that, I stand down from dialogue.

Short General Tips.

Rules of Grouping = Rhythm.

The Rule of three is an unbeatable formula for anything, more so in writing. If you use the Three in the overall structure of the book, in the structure of the chapter and finally in the structure of scenes (or beat) – you will have a very solid outline. Everything always has this strange phenomenon to happen in three stages. Three beats to make a scene. Triangles in love affairs. The Protagonist, the Antagonist and the woman they both want. Force A attack, force B defends, force C unexpectedly enters from the side-line. There is also another angle. Just when the reader gets into the rhythm of threes, you drop one, or two. It will cause a bit of confusion in the readers mind's ability to predict your story. It will also create some uneasy feeling, kind of like the dooming music in a movie. Warning something is coming up.

Write once, do not rewrite.

I found that every time I rewrite my story, the rewritten book is worse than the first. You can never have the flow, which you wrote in the first place, again. That is taking a step back again. You have to make your outlay good. The better you setup your framework, the better your story will flow in the first draft. Do not go back and change the dialogue, do not change the story. You can edit many times, but edit some basic grammar, edit the spelling, punctuations. Do not edit and rewrite the story – unless it is really bad. Even in the case where you think you really need to re-write a part of the story - read the whole book from start up to the point where you want to rewrite – that way you reduce the risk of losing the story flow.

Show do not Tell.

I know many people love to say this. I do not care what they think; I tell you it is BS. Sometimes you have to show, sometimes you have to tell and sometimes you have to let the readers mind create. Showing is slow, if you show too much you will bore the reader to death. However, if you only tell, the reader will not bound to the seat either. In general, there are three effects and it depends what your purpose in the beat is. Showing gives more detail but it slows the pace of the story down. Telling is more compact, less details but increases the pace of the story while leaving a little more to the intuition of the reader. Insinuating and Ignoring is leaving a seed as scene in the back of the readers mind while you enter into the real action. This later is good to use for creating suspense and mystery. Finally, there is the blender where you use a part from two or more of these Show or Tells.

Dialog Secret.

Do you really want to know the three biggest secrets of the best dialogues? Keep it short, simple, to the point. As with your sentences, the shorter, the faster. Longer dialogue is dangerous. It tends to become boring, very quickly.

Character Actions & dialogue.

When I am writing a scene, I like to have a photo of the characters who will act in that scene on view. That way I find it easier to maintain the 'voice' and personality of that character active.

Empty the Waste Water.

If you are just starting to write, or been dormant for a long time; I would suggest you freshen the words of your mind first. Strange nobody ever consider this in lectures. If you want your stories to flow out, you will need to open the channels to your mind – and imagination. In addition, you need to dispose of the old rotten stuff before you can write fresh. And, you need to practice. I do suggest you join this as part of your practice with the concepts in the first book of this series – Fast Writing.

There are two parts in this running in. First, you sit down and start writing – at least 50,000 words, no frame. Just place on paper everything and anything you want to write in a book. When finished – Delete it all. Do not even read it again. Just wipe it out from your mind.

The next part you start to design a book. Make a nice outline of the story you wish to tell. Create your characters, everything to the best you can. Use the Spinal cord structure and create at least 30 scenes – Chapters / spines. Take a day or two, no more. Then let go. Write your story. Your target is at least 30 chapters, each chapter at least two pages – 1,200 words. This will result in a book of maybe 60-pages, 35,000 words - a nice starter. Let it go and flow, from start to finish. Do not edit in-between. Do not worry about perfection at all. Just let it flow. This should not take more than three or four days (See book #1 about Fast Writing).

Next, you edit that piece you wrote. Do not worry about perfect language nor punctuation. Just edit it so you can understand your own story. See how you were writing. Make short notes on writing and editing items you need to keep in mind for future. Read this book again, after your first edit. Then go back over your whole book. Finally, use a Text to Speech reader and listen to your story. When you reviewed your work a few times and you feel ready to start writing – safe that piece in a boo-boo file somewhere or delete it.

Now you start for real. Your channels should be open. Begin to make an outlay of your story. Spend two or three days, even a week – but make it as complete as you can imagine. Think of options, variations, organs, nerves, bacteria and viruses. Create, be original.

When you ready, get your time reserved with a big "DO NOT DISTURB" sign and let go. I find it best to do between two and four hours per session, 10,000 to 30,000 words each. Make each chapter between 1,000 and 5,000 words. Contrary to most other people, I suggest you finish the chapter or beat at least. Next time you want to write – read at least the previous chapter through (To get in the flow and mood) before going on writing the new. A slight variation between chapters are not serious, but within the same beat – that might be disastrous.

The Magic of Three.

In the magic of three lies the secret of balance. When you are stuck in your writing, or when you design your story – always keep the Three-Magic in mind. Did you miss one of the magic options? This is where the Anatomy understanding will come in handy. Throw a virus in the plot or let a sheering pain shoot out from the kidney.

Million Word Tip.

Do not always use words in your outline. Use photos or images. See the Google Search section below. You can practice the technique of using photos to write. Remember the old saying "*A picture speaks a thousand words*"? When you build your story timeline, fill it with the 'organs of your spine' and then add images. Write about the image.

PART 2 - Writing Non-Fiction.

Can you use Google? I mean, really USE Google to get exactly what you want in a very short period.

How does the potential of writing a complete 150 page, 30,000-word Non-Fiction book on any particular subject sounds? Oh, did I mention <u>in less than one day</u>? At absolute no cost other than your time and internet access. Indeed, I did just that. From start to finish, I wrote a free book, using all the techniques explained in this "*Sell Your Dreams*" series.

This book will show you how to use search engines more effectively to collect information. It will show you even how to assemble a lot of text and images for your books.

There are different styles of writing non-fiction books. The one reads like a scientific paper, the other reads like an interesting subject. On the first side, it is pure fact-based strings of arguments; the other is an art. In the later, the writer presents the subject in such manner that every person can understand it – and wants to learn more. There should be three sections, Capture, Presentation and Conclusion. I cannot think why the presentation should be boring.

This is the Science of Non-Fiction writings, to present a factual story in such way that the reader is captivated. Gone are the days that a non-fiction writing should read like a work of literature. The content and explanation of your subject is more important than the actual grammar and sentence structures. Leave that for literature creators. Nowadays, even non-fiction, is a fluid form of art.

In this book, I will present you some of the ideas I learned about writing Non-Fiction fast, while maintaining factual integrity. In addition, we will look at various ways to collect information and create your basic non-fiction book, easy.

The world of the internet is dynamic. Everything is in constant change. That which worked three years ago, does not work effectively anymore. Not only on the wide scale, but more so in the sites like Amazon.com. During the first few months of 2016, there were some major changes. Many people lost out big time, because they were using 'systems' that was not so very honest.

There are some techniques, still in operation to this day, which allows an unfair advantage to certain kinds of authors and publishers. I will explain these in this book; though I do advice against apply them if you want to build an honest long-term business on solid foundations.

To write or to outsource.

A question only you can answer for yourself. In these modern days, we can write a book, by using various techniques, in less than one week. That is the purpose of this series I wrote, all about how to do it yourself with no or minimal expenses. In truth, not all books sell well. It is better to invest your sweat in your new business and make profit from the first sale than to outsource and have to sell hundreds of copies to get your investments back.

There are millions of books in the world. However, there is none, which is your perfect story. It is up to you, to write your story, as you want it to be. It is in your power to create your own unique story, let it flow from the deepest level in your spirit and mind. Write your Dream, Sell your Dream.

Search Engine Basics.

Do you really understand how to get that exact information which you are seeking without having to read thousands of useless links and pages? It is surprising to see how little people realize the power of search engines these days. Search Engines (Maybe we should say Search Robots) are able to find exactly what you are looking for. However, you need to be able to explain for them what you want. Then, how can you explain if you do not really know yourself what you are looking for?

I am doing a lot of internet research, have been doing it since 1996. Thus with more than twenty years of experience, I think I know what I am doing. Surprisingly, while researching info for this book, even I discovered some new methods. Great search features and options, which I will explain in this book.

I love reading, and more particular – I love doing wide research on a particular subject. Everybody knows Google. People say 'Google …' more often than 'Search for …'. Did you know there are other search platforms as well? Here is my selected list:

Bing & Yahoo – Bing is Microsoft based and provider of the organic (Organic is non-commercial) results to Yahoo. Bing currently dominates about 12% of the search market. Bing is good at using trends, based on your personalized results, to get your feeds. Yahoo; once upon a time, but they made some stupid mistakes in the early parts of this century. Presently Yahoo corners about 9% of the search market. Recently they did make some good changes and there is hope for this platform to revive. Personally, I have been using Yahoo since the days before Google and their latest improvements do rank them amongst the top three.

WebCrawler – An Ancient one. In the older terms, this is a Robotic Spider. Even their logo is a spider. WebCrawler literally goes into every nook and niche of all websites, systematically, and extract information from there, lock it in its web and digest it over time. It works two ways. WebCrawler combined top information from Google and Yahoo to give you quick surface results. On its own, it supplies deep information in return. To use WebCrawler effectively is a bit more complicated than other search engines like Google or Yahoo, but you can get info not always on the surface with other results.

Google – By any measure, the best-known Search Engine we have today. Mostly it is the only one people know about. Since it is the most widely used, easiest to apply – and the bigger portion of this book; I will only want to clarify why people should also consider using the other web search tools. I am sure this might come a shock to some. "*Google estimates that the Internet today contains about 5-billion Gigabytes of data, and claims it has only indexed a paltry 0.04% of it all.*" Hallo, Google does not even have 1% of the World Wide Web data in its files, yet.

Remaining bigger engines are Ask, AOL and WOW, each with less than 6% of the market. I am not using any of these anymore.

My personal favourite is Google, probably 97% of all my searches I am doing through Google. There was a bunch of new features added over this last few years. These make Google float way above the rest. If only, you can get rid of the Paid Results, however, it is not too difficult nor problematic.

In a this booklet I am going to share some of my experiences and techniques in using Google Search and some of the other extremely useful Google features. Together, it is actually surprising if you need any other software!

When doing research there are three major information platforms; the traditional text / websites, images and videos. In addition, there is news, maps and books.

Here is a double edge sword. If you know how to search with good strong keywords, you will also know how to get the right keywords for your book when you publish it. The most important item in your search is the keyword. Typically, you need to consider the issue on which you want to research, trim it down to the most relevant single word. That is your prime keyword. Then you take that keyword and run it through a Thesaurus, looking for applicable synonyms.

The very basic:

In the Google search bar, you type in your primary keyword. Immediately, as you enter the first character, and with each following that, there is a drop-down window with autosuggestions. This is powerful information. As you are typing, the algorithm is trying to predict your search – but that is not just out of a dictionary. It is listing the words with the most searches on Google records, starting with the characters as you are typing. However, if you did a lot of research on that particular keyword, it is also going to consider the words you used before – hoping to help you speeding up your typing.

Using a word I never used before as example; Gambia. The search options are Gambia- news, tourism and map. None of these is suitable for my quest. I just pressed Enter. This first thing to notice is how many results there are – at 192 million that is way too many to work through.

Gambia|

gambia tourism
gambia university
gambia wiki
gambia facts

About 192,000,000 results (0.58 seconds)

I definitely need to narrow it down. Go down to the bottom of the page. There is another window "*Searches related to Gambia*". This is giving the major phrases (also known as Long-Tail-Keywords) in relation to your original keyword search.

Searches related to Gambia

gambia **tourism**   gambia **islam**

gambia **university**   gambia **holidays**

gambia **wiki**   gambia **history**

gambia **facts**   gambia **islamic republic**

Now, maybe I just need general information about Gambia. I will right click on "Gambia Facts" and open in a new window. Do the same with "Gambia History" and "Gambia Wiki". Now I will have three windows open to go read. However, before I read, I want to see some images about the country.

Go back to the top of the page and right-click on 'Images', open that in another new window.

gambia

All   Images   Maps   News   Videos   More ▾   Search tools

About 192,000,000 results (0.51 seconds)

That new window is my starting point. Do note, when you open that window, there is a 'narrowing down' subsection. Google will list many images of Gambia, but you can select to only want a particular section ie. Tourism, or about the City, its people, etc. Then you click on that grouping.

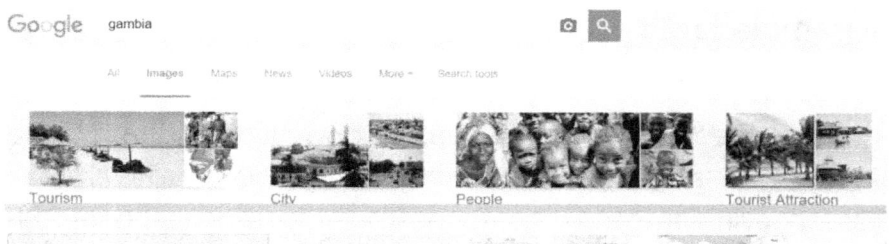

Scroll down through the images, when you see something that interest you, right click and open in a new window. At the bottom, there is an option to "Show more results" if you want to have more. This is a very fast way to learn about a new subject. When you have a number of interest images open in new Windows, then it is time to start learning.

Go through the images you selected and opened in new windows. It will look something like this:

On the left, big is the image you selected. To the right are eight additional images, somewhat related to the one you selected.

Notice the text "Gambia Group Tour Operators ..." That is the title for the website from where Google retrieved this big image. Below that, you can see the actual website URL and size of the image. Then there are two buttons "Visit Page" and "View Image". Visit page will go to the actual page, in this case 'arch-tours' as seen in the text above. View Image will open just the image in its biggest format on a page. We will get back to the images later. If you want, then right-click on the 'Visit Page", open in a new window. Next you look at the other related images. Click on each and view their descriptions, etc. I see for instance one city street scene and clicking on that the description is "Brikama Gambia" with their website. That sounds good. Right-click and open the page in a new window.

Now, I will look at those few detail pages and see if there is anything interesting. Any of that I will copy out into a word document i.e. Google Docks – or I will just copy the link URL and make a list of those with a very short description about the page.

Keep on going through the photos, their pages and view their pages. All the time you work form right to left – until you are back at the main image page No more interesting things. Close that and you are back at the main Google Result page with 192 million links.

It is quite surprising how much you can learn by just looking at photos or images. I facet, there is this wise saying "*A good image is worth a thousand words*". An option we are going to proof later in this book.

Now you have a much better idea about Gambia. You can spend time looking through some of the first results, link by link – or you can narrow the search down by adding long-tails to your keywords and search more. I might be considering writing a political book. Now that I know a little more about the country, I might enhance my main search with "Gambia Riots". I got 190 thousand results. I will then follow the same procedure. Go through the images, open in new pages, follow selective from there and work back to the original Search page.

Back on the main search page, I will then select videos. From that list (65,000) I will select a few videos and watch them.

All the time, when reading a web page, watching a video or looking at images; I will have a notepad. Make a note of any other keyword options that you might pick up. Later on, I will use these keywords to expand research into my subject.

Now that you have a good base to build upon, it is time to determine exactly what you wish to do with your results. For the sake of argument, I want to write a multimedia article about the Political issue in Gambia. I will need text, images and maybe video. For this purpose, it is important to know that everything on the internet falls into two main categories.

Copyrighted and 'Free Use'.

This is where Google shines above the rest again. Not everybody can jump on a plane to Gambia (or wherever) to take video and photos, thus we need to use whatever we can get from the Internet. It is critical that you use only that which you are legally allowed using.

Now is the time to create a more details map (or plan) of your intended book or article. In this case, I will say I am writing a short book.

I like the 'Table of Content' (ToC) feature in Google Docs. On the right side of my screen, I place a "Table of Content". This is an Add-on app you can activate in the 'Add-ons' menu. In my document I create the framework of my book, just type the headings you want, use the styles to make them headings. Then in the Table of Content (ToC) on the right click on the blue round arrowed button to update. You can do this all the time, at any time, as you continue to create your document. What is so nice here is that as you do your research, you can copy and paste selected text right into the intended heading or sub-headings.

As I see items, which I want to copy into my document, it is very easy with the ToC to jump to the right section.

<u>Back to Search.</u>

I used an ugly word for when talking of writing your own document. "**Copy**". That is dangerous, and it is unethical. How far you want to push the issue is up to you. I prefer to re-write all my content anyway, and not use copied words for words.

Regardless, there are even lots of text, which you can legally use. Finding out from all your research which you may use and which you may not use, is tenuous. Unless you knew that Goggle could do it for you, all ready and clean. You need to go to Google Advanced Search. At first, you will find the 'setting' option on the bottom right of your Google Search screen. Click on that and open "Advanced Search".

That will open the Advanced Search Screen. Here you can define your searched by various words, exact words, and excluding some words, series of numbers, language, region

(Country), etc. The last option reads "usage rights". Click on the down arrow and you have five options:

Not Filtered by Licence – All links, regardless of copyright or license.

Free to use or Share – Links that you may share, or copy from, but not for commercial purposes and it must be in the complete format, not modified.

Free to use or Share, even commercially – Links which you may use freely, even on commercial basis; but not modified. i.e. If there is a watermark or Photographers name, that has to go with the photo, you are not supposed to crop that off.

Free to use Share or Modify – You can share as is, or you can modify for yourself; but not commercial.

Free to use, share or Modify, even commercially – Free to do whatever you wish. (*You may notice that most of the results in this case are wikipedia related. We will come back to that option for writing books on later stage.*)

That is the basic guidelines for text searches. Now you can research, clip lots of info, compile your book and rewrite what you need to redo. You know also that you can copy even text as-is and use it if so you wish.

What about Images and Videos?

This is working the same. When you do your normal search, you are using the 'All' filter. Just on the top, you can click to filter only the images. On the menu bar on top there is the option "Search Tools". Click on it and you will get a menu of additional filters. Select the one suitable for your purpose. In addition, you can also select the size, colour, type of images to filter down to suit your requirements more.

There you are, advanced searching for information. Then narrow it down to text and images, which you can legally add into your publication, for sale or now. Remember you can also search for videos, a great mass of information to learn about the new subject. Then there are the News articles. Mostly news articles are copyrighted, but you can use the info and edit it nicely.

Wikipedia is a magnificent information source for compiling your book. They do have one important feature not often known.

UberSelect: http://www.ubersuggest.io

In my third book of this series, I talked about UberSelect a bit. That App is very useful to find additional keyword phrases for searching. Simply open the page and type in your main keyword. Then scroll down to see the list of words and additional words. You can expand until 5 words in each phrase.

Wikipedia.

Then there are the books based on internet-licenced content, which falls under the "Creative Commons", Public Domain, Free Content, etc. When I realized this, I was surprised to find thousands of books on Amazon.com which is nothing else than poorly complied Wikipedia source material. Then I took an in depth look at this concept.

I asked five questions, these are my findings.

1 - Is this legal? Yes it is. Provided you give recognition to the original Author.

2 - Is this acceptable? If you purely copy and compile a bunch or rubbish, no it is not. However, if you use the source material and you even just re-order them to create a reasonable value for the reader – yes it is acceptable. However, I advise you to maintain a low price tag.

3 - Does Amazon accept this? Indeed, to a great extent. See the section WikiPedia Books in Amazon.com.

4 - Can I sell my compiled book for money? Yes, you can. Provided you do credit the original authors of the pieces you use – and prevent Plagiarism.

5 - Is this ethical? For me, to copy with full credit to the original author – yes. To copy and not accredit the original author, that is wrong. However, personally I prefer to use the compilation as base of source material, but rather write my own content.

Before you can use this particular feature, you will first need to go to www.wikipedia.org and create your basic free account. Read the bulleted list of items to be acquainted to the basic rules and options. Lower down you may also notice other options which are available i.e. Wikimedia, Wiki-News, etc.

Then, on the left side you will see a menu bar. Look down to the section "Print/Export" and under that, there is "Create a Book". It is here that the fun in book writing can start. You can literally write a book of 100's of pages in just a few minutes. Maybe an hour if you attend to some details.

Weather you can ethically sell your Wiki-book is a grey area. The reason is that you are using complete articles from other authors, and information that is Public Domain. I do recommend you to build your basic book here, then export it and edit the whole book over with additional information. Do cite the names of authors whose articles you used as source references; do not cite 'wikipedia' as source.

Good news is that you can even order a complete printed book, which you can use as trophy on your bookshelf! However, that is not what we are interested in here. You can download your creation as one of two file types: As pure text only, no links, and no images. Alternatively, you can download as an e-book in PDF format. The text document you can use anywhere. For Google Docs, you will need to upload the text to your cloud. The PDF file you cannot open in Google Docs, thus you will need another editor i.e. MS-Word. As example, I did a complete Wiki book, downloaded to my MS-Word and transformed to a word document, ready to edit = 59,686 words on 158 pages; all in less than one hour. In addition, I did select the articles I wanted to include as my base.

When you click on the Create Book item, you will be presented with the "Manage Your Book" page. Give a title, sub-Title, select your paper size, for Table of Contents – pick Auto for now and make the book in one column. Next you start. Create your Chapter 1, and give it a descriptive name. That is all; you are ready to build your book.

Go to the top right, there is a search box. Start your searches with keywords. A tip: You can use the same keywords you already identified from Google searches. In the top centre of your screen is a box with three options. '+ Add' this page to your book, Show book (0 Pages) and suggest Pages. When you have a document which you want to include in your book, then simply click on the '+ Add'.

Once you have some pages in, you can use the 'Suggest pages" option to add more pages, or you can go back to the search box on top to search for other pages. Right at the bottom of the page are more additional options to help you in searching, or getting information.

Start using the multi keyword searches. For instance "Gambia Crime". That yields a number of pages, just like Google. You can check their short summary, if interested, right-click and open in new window. When you find more articles, simply 'Add' them on top. You cannot clip a part of an article. Can only do that when you downloaded your Wiki-Book and get to editing the book.

There are some other features you can use, though I find this more than sufficient to get a basic book foundation ready. What I normally do, when I copy text – like this from Wiki or other – and past them into a document / book as base, I highlight all the text in yellow. That way, I know it is copied and still need to be edited or rewritten.

The other way to do is by having your Google Docs open with a Table of Content on the side. As you are searching through Wiki, you can select and copy only portions of text, then go to the relevant chapter in your Docs book and paste there.

Public Domain in Amazon.com

If you change on the content of Public Domain books, according to Amazon rules – then your book is permissible, publishable and you can make money from it. Here are the rules from Amazon.com.

Selling content that is in the public domain is permissible through our program. We may request that you provide proof that your submitted material is actually in the public domain and may refuse public domain content already available through our Program or available through other retail sites.

In order to provide a better customer buying experience, our policy is to not publish undifferentiated versions of public domain titles where a free version is available in our store. We consider works to be differentiated when one or more of the following criteria are met:

• (Translated) - A unique translation

• (Annotated) - Contains annotations (unique, hand-crafted additional content including study guides, literary critiques, detailed biographies, or detailed historical context)

• (Illustrated) - Includes 10 or more unique illustrations relevant to the book

Books that meet this criteria must include (Translated), (Annotated), or (Illustrated) in the title field.

For example, "Pride and Prejudice (Annotated)" is acceptable, while "Pride and Prejudice (with an Introduction by Tiffany Gordon)" is not. The product description must also include a summary of how the book is unique in bullet point format at the beginning of the product description (maximum 80 characters).

While it is possible that other features will make books unique, we consider only public domain titles with the criteria noted above to be differentiated. Examples of some features we do not consider to be differentiated include a linked table of contents, formatting improvements, collections, sales rank, price, and freely available Internet content.

WikiPedia Books in Amazon.com

If it comes from Wikipedia, as far as Amazon.com is concerned – it is public domain. However if you have a large number of books, poorly compiled and at expensive prices – there will be complaints. Complains makes Amazon unhappy. They will remove your books on that basis alone. Emily Smith had more than 1,600 WikiPedia compiled books at one stage, but the reviews were very bad. Most of the related books were sold at prices around US$ 20.00. Since Amazon trimmed her books down and now, she remains with just over 100 titles.

The publisher – Emereo – had more than 23,000 Wiki Articles out as books. Emereo originally used the pen name of Emily Smith – now they use many different fake pen names. Yet, just about all their books are compilations from Wikipedia and similar websites. Currently they have more than 11,000 titles.

There is another 'author' - Philip M. Parker. He wrote a computer software that takes WikiPedia articles and converts it to eBooks, which he publishes on Amazon.com. Currently he has more than 130,000 eBooks on sale. You can watch a video of his system here:

https://youtu.be/m8WuGKyBR90

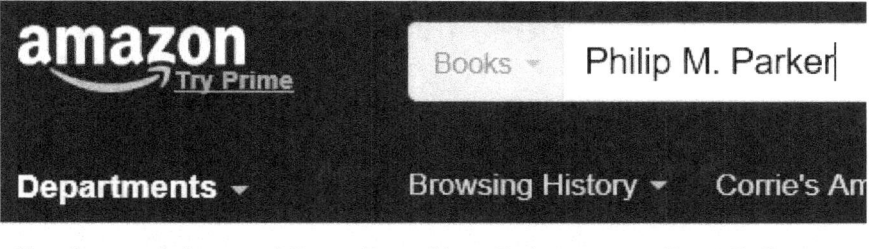

1-12 of 134,047 results for **Books** : "Philip M. Parker"

Getting Ideas for your Books.

What can I write about? This should never be a problem for any writer. It is just a matter of opening your senses and imagination. If you experienced this problem, right there where you sit now – take a look around you. Make a short note of what you see, smell, hear and feel. Done.

On my desk is my computer, a pen and a roll of toilet paper (a bit of running nose). Can I use these as base for a book? YES! Let me explain.

<u>The pen.</u> I can write about the history and science behind the pen. From where did it came? Millennia ago the writing instrument was a rock used to chisel images on cave wall. A whole non-fiction story unfolding. Alternatively, I can write about the pen and ink bottle that was used to write the American Constitution. Where, Who, What, When, Why – and How. I can turn that into a Historical Fiction book. Or you can use the pen as weapon to kill a well-protected person. Maybe build a small gun into it (such has been done). Murder Thriller.

<u>Toilet paper.</u> Non-fiction we can write about paper history, or the forests that use to supply paper. We can run a fiction story about an activist that wants to legalize cannabis plants for making paper – true anyway. How about a man sitting on a toilet at home, designing a magnificent space engine with notes on toilet paper squares. Yes, in truth I know a person who designed a fantastic concept on toilet paper while he was sitting on the toilet. That construction is still in Pattaya to this day, and those pieces of toilet paper are framed – inside this person's guest toilet!

You can just go walking, use your phone or camera and shoot many photos. When back at home, take a good look and imagine a story behind any one photo – or combine a number of photos to a single story.

Log onto your <u>Facebook</u> account. Look at the posts other people made, note those that have plenty likes or comments. Take that and create a non-fiction or fiction story around that concept.

Use Google's "I feel Lucky" feature and page through ideas, photos, videos and whatever until you see something you like. Expand on that.

Above in this book in my Beat Sheet sample you see an image of a Mars Rover. I took that image and am now building a whole novel around that. Soon I will publish "Expansion" – it all from just that single original photo.

Ideas are there, all around you, everywhere. It is only for you to train your mind, observe and notice these ideas and then use your imagination for expanding the concept to a potential story.

I wish you good luck and happy writings.

Sell Your Dreams
Fast Writing & Editing

Corrie Lamprecht

Introduction.

Are you frustrated of the many long hours it takes to write an article, or a book? Have more ideas to write than time available?

In this book I am going to show and guide you in the latest technologies. You will learn how to use them very effectively. In fact, so effectively that you can take any idea of a story from start to published in less than 24-working hours. And start to make money.

Today I am happy to type an easy 10,000 words in one day, with reasonable spelling and grammar. If I am pressing, I can do more than 40,000 words on a good day. In 6x9" or A5 book size, with an 11 pitch font; that translates to something between 50 and 200 pages per day.

Unfortunately it was not always like that.

Even at the beginning of 2016 it took me 3-months to finish "*The Emerald Buddha*". The second book "*eBook Guide for non-Americans*" was a bit faster at about 2 months.

The first book in this series "*Sell Your Dreams*" took me three days, from planning, researching, writing, editing and ready for publishing. Graphics and images – all done by myself.

I wrote my first book way back in 1994, it was a LOT of work at the time. I knew my subject very well but still spent months on additional research. The book was "Aromatherapy", all about the history, how to make the oils and massage techniques. That book included a list of 347 essential oils, with chemical constituents, healing properties, blending and applications.

I worked on that book for more than 6 years; a time when an 80286 computer was high tech and MS-Windows 3.1 was the WOW factor at computer shows. WordStar was the editor of choice. I can vividly remember the package was 16 black five-inch floppy disks and three, thick printed books. Another big hit was off course in the build in spell checker.

When the book was finished, I printed it all out on my dot-matrix printer; as was required at that time. It was over 1,400 pages double-spaced and I hit the sidewalks of Pretoria and Johannesburg. I started with a feather light step and big dreams...selling 1000's of copies. Every day the sales dream shrank and my shoes got heavier. That book was good. Nope, it was very good. It was never printed; nothing sold and over the years, thanks to countless computer crashes and theft – I only have about 10% of that book on my back-up drives.

Around 2002, while in Saudi Arabia, I was asked to analyse some water treatment technology and present a paper on my findings. My problem was that always I tend to overdo everything; too good, too big, too much detail. Anyway, I wrote a report, which was substantial.

I realized it was good enough to print in book format. "The Properties of water and Purification treatments". It was an A4 sized book with 250 pages and hundreds of sketches done in Corel Draw. It took me four months, full time, to complete. When I came back to Thailand, I e-mailed copies to a few publishers; hoping they would be keen to publish it. Nada. Nothing. Zilch. About a month ago, I looked at parts of that book that are still on old hard drives … it is very good, very detailed. *(I might review and re-edit it and publish it as an eBook.)*

For the second time in my life, no publishing and no sales.

That was it for me; hundreds of hours and begging to get a book sold. Over these past few years, a number of people kept on prompting me to write books, I know quite a lot, and I can write on many subjects. I just ignored it; I have tried twice - no more. Then last year (2015), a friend opened my eyes to other possibilities.

Now I am happy. Very happy. I can write a book. Very quickly. Now I am talking of hours, no months or years anymore. I trust you will find this book very useful.

Chapter 1 – Getting Ready.

Everybody has dreams.

Everybody has ideas.

Everybody has something, to share.

Last night I thought about my book, which is just about ready for publishing, but I am not feeling too happy about the title *"eBook Guide – For those living outside of the USA"*.

Somewhere along the night these exact words came to my mind "Make money with your dreams". I thought by myself "Now that is a good title to use". In the morning I thought, rather than change the name - why not write a new very short book about making money from your dreams. Here I am.

This is going to be an exercise for me and for you. I am going to keep a record, here in writing, of time and the exact things I do. Thus, it may help other aspiring writers to try a new life. I will also record some video and make that into a presentation part of this document.

It is now Tuesday 14 June 2016 and 06h12. Just finished my morning routine – Coffee, e-mails and check the news. I started to look into Google Docs first time ever, about 24 minutes ago.

Maybe the title should be "How to write a book"; but then I think you might not read this. You see this is the first lesson - a catchy original name is so important.

There are some tools you will need. Without this off course, you cannot do what I will share with you. First you need some sort of a brain, most people does have excellent brains. Then you need some part of your body to convert your mind into words. Sometimes it is fingers, but not always. There are other options like a tongue or lips. I have seen people writing book – with no arms nor hands. Finally (for now), you might need a sort of electronic device – this could be a computer, a smart phone or even a sound recorder. That is all.

Some other things you might need later to finally 'Sell your Dreams', but we will cover that in time. Often you can simply borrow a computer, use an internet café or get a friend to help, no serious obstacle there.

Now, please do keep in mind – I am picking on the keyboard like a bird. Just a few fingers jumping all over the place; some day, I will sit down and reset my mind with a proper typing course. On second thoughts, maybe not. That is Old School.

I am going to show you what I do, how I do and what I use. This is a photo of my computer and my comfortable writing chair.

For parts of my normal writing, I use Microsoft Word 2013 - but you can use any other program. Open Office is a good freeware program. It is free and it is quite similar to MS-Word.

As we go through this whole creation sequence, I will use only free software. This will all be new to me, therefore a bit of a time handicap. I want to see (and proof) that one can get all along creating and publishing e-books without any big expenses; and in relative short time.

We will be using Google Docs Voice for dumping the words from our brains onto the computer. Thus, as I am comfortably sitting back in my chair, I type with my tongue. My target is to see if I can write this book in less than one week from start to sale.

The first objective is just talking into the microphone. Hey, did I mention you could even do it on your smart phone? Yes, they have excellent dictating software. All that time waiting for a bus, sitting on the train or biting your nails in a traffic jam – use that to convert your ideas into words.

While on this point, I find it very useful and amusing when sitting somewhere and dictate whatever you see and hear, right there into your phone. It might look crazy to other people but what do I care. It is my dream. I am the boss.

Since my accent is non-English speaking and maybe my tongue and lips are a bit funny shaped, the dictation software sometimes finds it very difficult to understand me. Hey, but it is fun. Sometimes I burst out in fits of laughing on what the thing is typing. Do not worry about editing exactly; just get the general words flowing from mind to high tech 'paper'. Once you have the whole story transcribed from your mind into readable words, much later – then you can start editing and polishing it up.

Why do I not make a video instead of all the efforts of writing? Well, videos can sell, but will not really make you money. Videos do take a lot more time to create, edit and it is a steep learning curve. Anyway, we will get to the video making later on. For now, just remain with writing a book – that can sell better and can convert your dreams into pocket cash.

We need to get our dream converted to words. For that, I will use Google Docs and it has a built-in 'voice typing'. Remember you do not need to do exactly as I suggest, neither do have to use exactly the software I recommend. This is only suggestions, and at the same time, I want to see how far I can get a book produced without using any of my usual commercial software packages.

To start with, you need to have Google Chrome as browser on your device *(by device I mean computer, notebook, tablet or smart phone)* and you will need a Google e-mail account. This is important, as we will make a lot of use of the (Free) Google system throughout this whole process. If you do not have, then get onto your internet connection, go to www.google.com and install Google Chrome browser - and register for Gmail.

Open up Google browser, type in the search "google docs" and look for "Google Docs – create and edit …" as per the snip below. Do take note; Google Docs will only work with Google Chrome as browser.

Microsoft (and other editors) does have some dictation abilities but I found Google Voice Typing is many magnitudes better.

Google Docs - create and edit documents online, for free.
https://www.**google**.com/**docs**/about/ ▾
Create and edit web-based **documents**, spreadsheets, and presentations. Store **documents** online and
access them from any computer.
You've visited this page 4 times. Last visit: 6/13/16

Google Drive
Store any file. Drive starts you with 15
GB of free Google online ...

Google Slides
With Google Slides, you can create,
edit, collaborate, and present ...

Google Sheets
With Google Sheets, you can create,
edit, and collaborate ...

Google Forms
Collect and organize information big &
small with Google Forms ...

More results from google.com »

Next you will see the welcoming screen, click on "Go to Google
Docs". A new screen will open and you will see a few document
templates. Click on the first one with the big + sign. Later you
can create templates and pre-formats but we will leave that for
now.

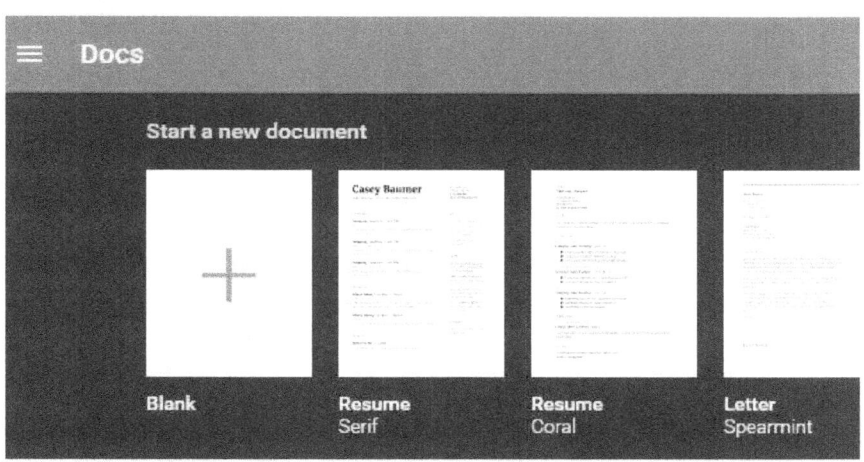

Smart Phone: *You need to browse with Google chrome, then
search for Google Docs, download and install the app. You will
need to sign in with your Google Gmail account. Next, in your
mobile device you need to go to the Settings, look for 'Language*

and Input' click on that and make sure 'Google Voice Typing' option is ticked (available). Also, check your Text-to-Speech setting to be Google Text-to-Speech engine and speed rate is Normal. You can play around with these options to see which is best suited for your speech pattern. You should then see a small icon on you keypad. (Usually on the button just left from the SpaceBar.)

Now you will see a new blank document. Guess what, you are all ready and set to go. Here is another reason why I like this setup. The moment you registered for Google, you also received 15 Gb of cloud storage space – for free.

Working with Google Docs will safe your work all the time right there in your Cloud storage – and you can just go on working nearly unlimited on any device. Without any problem, I can sit here working on my computer; get up and go out. While driving I can talk to my hands-free phone – dictating. All the time working with my mobile phone, right on the same document as if no interruption. It always keeps your document saved. You can edit your documents off line, and then as soon as you connected, it will upload to the cloud storage again.

OK, now you have a new blank document in front of you. Next, get your microphone ready. I recommend you using a good quality microphone, though I am just using a cheap multimedia condenser microphone; and it is still working OK. A better microphone quality will result in less errors with the Voice Typing.

On the title bar, look for Tools and click to open the drop-down list. Click on "Voice Typing". This will place a Microphone icon next to your work page (on mobile phones it will be in the keyboard). If it is the first time, your setup might ask permission to use the microphone. Agree to that. Next, your anti-virus software might also want to confirm you wish to open the Microphone and explain some safety issue. Agree to that also.

A few 'strange' things will happen in the background. As you type (or dictate) the document will keep on saving it in your Cloud Space. (Notice on the right side of the Menu Bar). It will be good to give your document a new name. Go to File > Rename. Let us call this first one "Dreaming".

Let us dig in right away. It is Tuesday morning 07h15 and I switched my computer on nearly 2 hours ago. Overall, not too bad for 2 hours – considering I also had to learn the basics of Google Docs.

Are you ready? Google Docs open with Dreaming file name, microphone in front of you, switched on. Nice and quiet, no big machine noise like air-conditioner or kids playing …

I made a video for this section. You can click HERE or else need to type this into YouTube: **(https://youtu.be/4lNL-Riu7kk)**

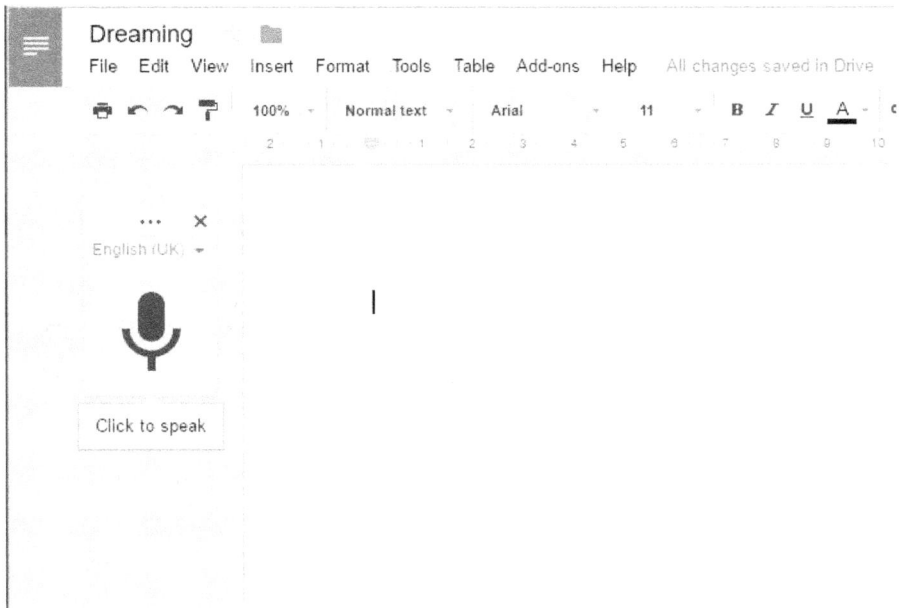

By now you might have realized there are some issues like missing capital letters and punctuation marks. There are just a few voice commands you need to know right now. You can find the whole description by going to the menu "Help > Docs Help > type 'Voice' and click on 'Type with your voice' ". You can learn all you need there.

For now, test and play with your voice typing. Speak some words and then use the following commands when appropriate: Comma, period (or full stop), new line, new paragraph.

This is the most difficult aspect to overcome. Tell your story AND use words to command punctuation and formatting. To Voice type the following line:

"Hallo. My name is Corrie. I am here to show you, how *to sell your dreams*".

It will be voice typing like "hallo period … my name is corrie period … i am here to show you comma … how to … apply italics … sell your dreams … italics … period … new paragraph …" (Where the … indicating a short pause).

Right, click on the microphone and start playing around with this wonderful toy. Take your time, see how your voice and the microphone can adopt, get comfortable with this new system. Mouse and Microphone is a nice combination. Notice the auto-corrections. Try to speak a bit faster, slower and notice how it will affect your Voice to Text. Find your own sweet spot, consider also the effect time for punctuation commands. In time, it will become like a second nature, easy.

In fact this Voice to Text feature of Google Docs is more accurate than most of the similar kinds of programs – even expensive ones – that I looked at over this past year. When you feel a bit more comfortable with the first round of experimenting – we can go on.

Oh yes. Did I tell you there are a large number of language options? Yes, you can even 'write' in Afrikaans, Thai, Chinese, Greek … just about any language you wish. The Thai language seems to do well, but when using Afrikaans I find the punctuation marks not working well. On the Menu bar, go to File > Languages to try another language for voice typing.

As if that is not enough, you can also translate your document into other languages. However, usually the translation is not perfect; you will need to do quite a bit of editing. On the Menu Bar, go to Tools > Translate.

Since we are targeting a novel type story rather than non-fiction, we might need to use only a few commands.

A few personal tips. If you speak continuously, the words are typed out, even the commands. Give a bit of a pause (Not too long) before you give a command like 'Full Stop or New Line'. Play a bit around with the pauses between voice typing and commands, try various commands – until you are more comfortable with the basic commands.

The full list of Voice typing commands are at Menu>Help>Docs Help – then in search type "Voice commands" and click on "Type with your voice".

In an attempt to understand you better, the Voice to Text feature is making extensive use of Auto-Correction. In other words, they correct their most likely miss-understandings of your speech. This you will sort out later when editing. While dictating you will not see everything of all words; until you pause or say the commands like comma or period.

Do not look at the screen and try to read as you dictate. It may confuse the flow of your story. Just keep a slight corner of the eye on top of the screen for in case there is a problem with the microphone or the typing stopped. I like to sit back and talk, thus not reading the words, but I can see if there is a failure.

Once you have done about one page, stop the microphone and just read the piece, correct the obvious mistakes. Here your purpose is purely to ensure that you will be able to know the storyline when you get to the editing phase.

Do use short rapid sentences rather than long paragraph lines – this makes it easier when dictating and fixing errors.

Just talk at normal voice, normal speed. Speak your words clearly. You will be surprised to find how little time it takes to do a page or two.

It is now Tuesday 14 June 2016 - 00h10. I have done 8 pages with 2,158 words. This was a lot of thinking, looking and playing with Google Docs myself – first time I used it. Now I need to go for a walk, breakfast and some things to do. Will be back later today.

A short novel on most eBook sites are somewhere between 5,000 and 20,000 words. A reasonable book is between 40,000 and 120,000 words.

Just for the sake of curiosity, I start all over on a new document and told a story as if to my son. It took 6 minutes to dictate 1,464 words. Then I edited the five pages for phrases, spelling, quotation marks and punctuation. In all it took me 21 minutes to dictate, edit and basic format five pages of a story. At this time, it implicates that a reasonable 5,000 word Dream Story could be completed in one day!

All I need you to do is just dictate at least two pages of text. Do not concern about exact spelling, language or punctuations. Just get some long text on. Tell a story for yourself. If you find there is a sudden blank in your mind, do not worry. It is normal.

Well, it might be a modified book version of 'Stage fright' – we will work around that. You can always take a printed book and just read a page or two into your Dream Document.

By the way – you might find the Quotation marks difficult. I fail, thus I need to edit them into my document during the editing.

While you are practicing, let us review some interesting facts.

The average printed novel is between 80,000 and 120,000 words, and those thick door blockers sometimes get up to 300,000 words. In general, those authors work a year or more on each book.

The part time writer types between 1,000 and 3,000 words per day; usually during something like 6 hours. People spend up to three times that long to edit and fix and about the same time to prepare for publishing an eBook.

The average eBook (fiction novel) is less than 10,000 words (40 pages). In general, the story is not drawn-out-to-make-pages, but rather short, easy and quick to read. Typical your 'read-one-book-a-day' range. There are no restrictions at all and no set law anywhere. Generally, it is recommended your eBook should be more than 5,000 words. However, the most important issue is the content, not the words. People want to get value for their money, and they want to enjoy reading your fiction book.

eBooks in general sell for cheap. Write an eBook in one day, spend a few days on editing and spend two day on marketing. Sell for relative cheap, I am talking of prices between US$ 0.99 up to US$ 2.99. Done, next one. In a year, with some marketing, that eBook could earn you as little as US$ 200 or as much as US$ 10,000 – and yes, some people do sell a short eBook for even more than that income per year.

The way we are going to do it is somewhat different and a lot faster. A fun fact. With this system, I am showing you here, your first book may take a month to get on sale. Your second book will take no more than 60 hours of work. By the time you do book number three, it should be comfortably possible within 24-hours of working.

Here is the main point. When you type with your fingers, it is much slower than your thoughts, thus your brain wanders around. This cause confusion in the actual writing flow. Therefore, a lot of editing comes into play when you read the book for yourself the first and second time. Here, while the actual typing is somewhat confusing, your 'talk' is already cutting out a lot of 'story-flow-editing'. Much reduced editing time. Sit back with a good microphone, relax and tell your story. You will be surprised to see it takes just a few hours to write a fairly good size eBook.

Please do experiment with Google Docs and its build in Voice typing; using what we learned until now. I need you to be comfortable. For a new user, maybe one full day will be more than enough. When you are ready, we can go on to Chapter 2.

Chapter 2 – Workspace.

For our book, we are going to start with three objectives.

The eBook is an electronic file the buyer can download and read on his preferred electronic device. In this case your fonts, sizes, colours, etc. does not mean anything at all, and the reader can pick whatever he wants from his device. As for your writing, it is the simplest you can imagine.

Next in line is **the pBook** – Print-on-Demand. Here you can do a lot more nice editing, etc. BUT, we are not going to do that in this experiment, simply because we will use the build in features from our uploading session. Thus, for all practical purposes, our eBook format above is already sufficient.

The last one is **the PDF file**. For a novel kind of book, this is a waste of time – just remain with eBook since it can be converted to pdf. The PDF structure is more adoptable for other kinds of books where you will incorporate text and many images. PDF format is perfect for educational, children books, etc.

To be acceptable for all of these three formats, we just need to make a few small changes in the Google Docs setups. I made a short video about this setting up; you can link to it from my website.

As you see below, I inserted some images. During the Voice typing, I just make a note where I want the image and add it later during editing. As example "new paragraph … insert image about page setup here…period…new paragraph".

From the Menu bar go to File > Page Setup. Edit the page settings to be Portrait, A5 (or 6x9") and all the margins 1.5 cm (1/2"). You do not really need to change the page settings; you can just use normal A4 paper – since the conversion will change paper according to the reader's preference and device. However, I like to have a better view of what the en book might look like.

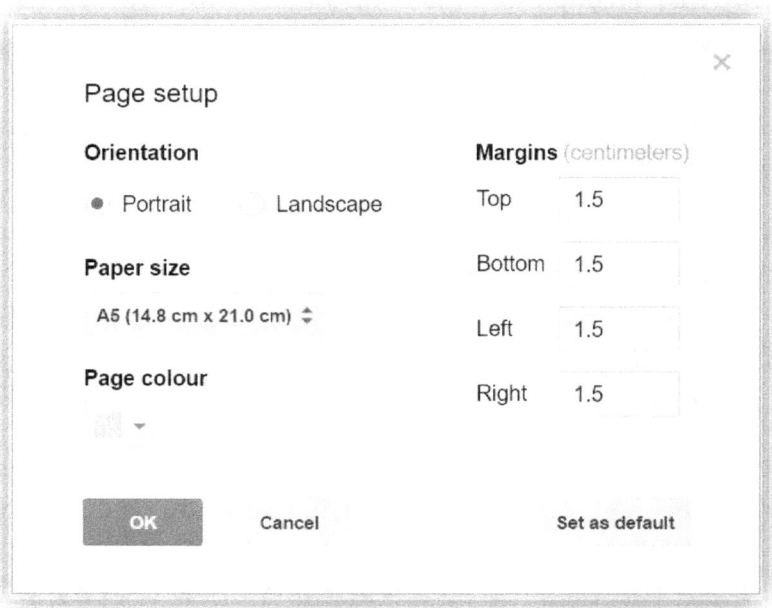

In the Menu>View, see that you have Print Layout, Show Spelling Corrections selected.

The next sounds a bit complicated, but if you watch this books linked video from my web page, you will understand better. Only use the Styles in formatting your eBook. Generally, which work on most if not all platforms is:

Use only a standard font like Times New Roman or Arial. Size does not really matter, but I prefer to work with text size at 11. Justification must always be either Left or Centre. Do not use Full Justified since the extra spaces can cause havoc on some readers.

Only use Normal Style throughout your document, changing to other Styles, especially embedded in the same paragraph will cause problems. Once you are more experienced, you can watch and read up on this somewhat controversial subject. If you need to use more than one type of style, I suggest you watch the very informative videos on YouTube.com about writing eBooks.

Generally, you can (or should) use Chapters to break the book into some sections. For that, you always use Heading Style 1, for sub-chapters use Heading Style 2 and for other use Heading Style 3. Do not use more than three levels of Headings; often the conversion software will ignore them.

To change the Styles in Google Docs, you will first need to write and format it on your page, and then you select the applicable area and update the related Style. As example, go to the top of a new page. Type the word Chapter and enter. Now go back to the 'Chapter', select the whole word, click on the Styles block in the formatting bar (#6 from Left). Click on Heading 1. You will see the 'Chapter' word changed to a bigger format. Keep the whole word selected and on the Format Bar click on Underline and Centre. This will move the word to the centre of the page and underline it. Next, click on the Line Spacing > Custom Spacing. Make Line spacing 1.1, Paragraph Before 0 and After 6. Apply. Now select the word 'Chapter' again, click on the Styles menu, go down to the Heading 1 and click on the right arrow and select "Update Heading 1 to match".

The others options are not important, for now. Everything else is optional, however – Keep it Simple. The more complicated and fancy you make your formatting, the more problems you may get with posting it to multiple sites for sales later. One important issue – you have to, as in must, use the Styles setups to do your formatting. Do not format 'on site' from the format bar.

Chapter 3 – Writing.

Are you ready to type your dream?

Then clear the screen and go for it. Put this book aside and get going on you telling me about your dream, or your story. Let us target a very small book, just for the sake of learning. Go for about 6,000 words, about 27 pages. How to know? On your top menu bar, go to Tools > Word count. It will tell you how many words you have and how many pages.

Check it through once only, if it is scrappy – then print it out, use a highlight pen and paint the good parts. Do not worry if you feel it is not good. I re-wrote all books a few times – and so does even the best of highly successful authors. It is the same as when a baby starts to walk, lots of falling down. Just keep on doing it, soon you will find it all comes automatic. Moreover, it will become like second nature and very easy. Tomorrow, you take the old book, read it two or three times, note the highlights, make notes in the sideline. Then, using that old copy, you sit back and tell the same story again, more balanced.

When you feel reasonably happy with the results, then it is time to start editing. You can still use the Voice feature, but I find the normal typing a bit better, faster and much easier. Normally I copy the text out to MS-Word and finish it off there. For this publication, I decided to do it all right along your side – in Google docs.

As a curious note, on a very good day I used to type around 5,000 words. That took me just about 12 hours. With Google Docs, I did 10,000 words in less than 3 hours of speaking. Amazing, I literally ran out of active brain cells for my Voice to Text story!

Here is a nice experiment; you will probably use it many times once you see the results. Take your tablet or phone and go somewhere where there are some people or some action. Pick a nice observation spot, relax and feel your environment.

Now open your device and start Voice to text, as if you are explaining everything to a friend on the other side of a phone. Tell them what you see, what you hear, what you feel. See how people walk, what they do. What clothes are they wearing, how do they interact with others around them. Tell what you are feeling, the wind, the sounds, the smells.

Next you can try and watch say a couple; make up a story about them. Play around with the First Person and also in the Third person. Tel it as if everything you experience around you – is your own experiences and observations.

"I see a man coming in my direction on a bicycle. He is riding very fast. Oh my God, there is a kid running in front of him. They crashed. I hear the screams, the little boy's mother come running up. I grabbed my bag and walk closer to see if there is anything I can help with."

Then change the story, tell it as if somebody else is describing it, and you are just a part of the scene. "He is walking down the road, isolated in his own thoughts. Aimless he kicked at a stone in front of him; it rolled to the middle of the road. A car is approaching from the back, driving very fast. The tyre of the car shot the stone up and right into the side window of a parked car. It shatters, setting the alarm off. The man stopped. His face filled with fear, he seems distressed. Then he hears the police sirens, turned around and quickly run around the corner."

Once you develop this habit of actually observing your environment, and talking about what you see – you will be amazed to find the results in your writing. You will find it easy to build characters. Listening to what and how people say things will diversify your dialogues.

A lot can be observed in a crowd. In time you can actually find so much fun doing this, you will have a whole library of clips to use in putting a future novel together. Hey, you will not even look out of place, draw no attention. Everybody is talking on their phones!

Chapter 4 – Editing.

We are going to edit our dream story a few times. It may seem a lot, up to you. However, I did find there is good madness in this chaos. Every time you edit, you get to clear out some mistakes, make the story better. Above all, your whole eBook is going to look - and read - better.

First Edit:

Just read the story, aloud, to yourself, alone. You can pause and edit the very bad places; particularly where the Voice Typing did not understood you well. Do not worry about perfection now.

Second Edit:

Read through your whole book from first to last word. Check for spelling, basic punctuations, quotation marks, sentence structures, etc. Rephrase some pieces, use build in editors and spell checkers.

Third Edit . . . *until you are perfectly happy*.

Here we start to apply the new technology again. In your Google Chrome, go to your photo on right top corner. Click > My Account > Account Preferences > Accessibility put 'Screen Reader' ON. Now, back in your Docs, there should be another menu item 'Accessibility; on the right. If not press Ctrl+Alt+z to activate. Now you can select a part of the text, press Ctrl+Alt+x to let the computer read it back to you. Do this twice. One time you read with him/her, second time you only listen.

Edit using Text to voice.

This is the reverse of what we have done while writing. I find this extremely useful. You can use the Text to Speech in your

Google Docs or directly on your Google Drive (Where this Google Docs documents are saved). It is useful.

The other option is to download your file in PDF format, then use the Adobe PDF reader to read your document aloud. In Adobe PDF reader, open your PDF document, then on the menu bar go to View > Read Out Loud. In your document you need to select an area (using mouse) and it will read that part out.

My personal preference is to download the file in MS-Word format, then open it in my MS-Word. There I can have the document read to me – while editing some sections on the fly. I included a short clip of doing this in the video.

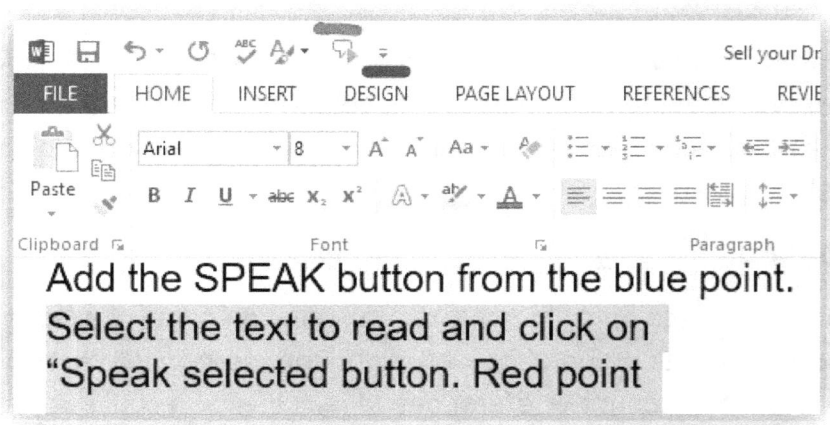

Add the SPEAK button from the blue point. Select the text to read and click on "Speak selected button. Red point

In MS-Word you will need to add the "Speak Selected Text" menu button first. On the most top bar of your menu bars, click on the little down arrow (Blue marked) and select "More Commands" then "Quick Access Tool Bar". In the first option bar (Now shows Popular Commands), click down and select "All Commands". Scroll down to "Speak", click and then click on "Add" between the two columns. Now your top bar menu will show up like this image. Select text in your work piece and click on the "Speak Selected Text" button – the one under the Red line. This feature is extremely useful during the final editing of text.

While the lady is reading your text, listen to her and read it on your screen at the same time. If there is an error, you can correct it without interrupting the reading. If big, the stop the reading, edit the piece and then select again to read.

I find this an amazing tool. Often I have some typical errors, like fingers. I will for instance type 'form' instead of 'from', or the auto correct will type 'and' instead of 'an'. When you read the text yourself, these errors mostly go un-noticed simple because your brain knows what is supposed to be there.

The other problem is that when you type and read your text, you already know what is supposed to be there, so you do not really 'proof-read'.

By having the text read back to you, you can hear it when another person speaks – surprisingly how many errors you pick up there.

Do this editing until you are happy. I usually take about half a page or maybe one page at a time. Amazing how quickly you identify some errors in grammar, text, words choices, etc. You can change the voices also, that makes the story not boring – actually quite interesting. You can also use other Google Apps. Personally I like the free TTSReader; only problem is you need to copy and paste the text.

While on this reference to additional help during editing, there are also some nice add-ons you can use in Google Docs. Go to your Google Docs menu and select Add-ons, go down to "Get Add-ons ..." There are many Apps you can add in, depending on just what you like. Most are free, some has a free trial period.

Thesaurus
617,834 users

I have added three which I find very useful.

- SAS Writings Advisor; Free.

- Thesaurus; Free

- Pro-Writing Aid; Basic free, Pro version US$ 40 per year.

Keep in mind, these do not write your text, neither will they do automatic fixing. They merely make suggestions to you. You, as writer, has to decide what, how and where you wish to change.

Chapter 5 - Publication Edit.

This is the Golden law; "You have no option, follow the rules, keep it simple and short". For this first book, we write the simplest book possible. Your dream. A fiction novelette. There is no index, funny text, graphics, fact checking, tables or any other complicated things to clutter the book. Just lots of words and a few chapter heading to give break times for the reader.

In fact, you should have used only one normal font and one Style type of header for chapters – that is it.

First, you need to go through the whole book – punctuation. Forget about the story; concentrate on the comas, periods, quotation marks, paragraphs, etc.

A few thing to keep in mind;

There should be only one space between sentences in the same paragraph; unlike the British/South African way of double space bar. Took me a long time to get that out of my mind.

There should be no more than one open line anywhere between paragraphs; preferably none. The one that generates when you press Enter at the end of your paragraph; it is not a full open line.

Check that you have a full stop (period) at the end of every paragraph and no space following that. Check your quotation marks. A few simple rules – an open quote must have a closing quote, within the same paragraph. Check the proper placements of punctuation marks – inside and outside of the quotes.

Check your chapter headings; paragraph formats i.e. justifications, spaces between them, etc. When you done and feel good –then read the whole book, slowly again.

Title Page.

Now you need to go back right to the beginning, if you do not have it or did not use a template - Insert a new first page. That will be your title page. Here you only write the name of your book, your author name and copyright description. See the first page of this book for a sample.

Do make sure you add a link to your website and/or Facebook page. We will get back to this later in the marketing section.

Preface.

It is up to you if you want to include this in your book, I usually do. It is usually the same text I am using to introduce my book to potential buyers. In other words, it tells the reader what this book will be about. We can compare this to the back page you find on older printed books.

Just write enough to tell the reader what your book is about, but do not tell them the whole story. Generate curiosity. Here you need them to develop a desire to read the rest of your book. In fact, this is the second most important sales point for selling your dream.

Last Page.

Still inside your covers. Here you can introduce yourself as Author – that is part of the marketing strategy of your future books. You can also introduce a "Look out for ..." about your next book. By this time, I hope you already started on your next book. Most important, do add links to your Facebook page and to your Web site.

I already finished the second book of this series. That is quite a bit more about the marketing of your book, in particularly on Amazon.

Chapter 6 – The Cover Page.

Now; this is the most important part of your whole physical book when coming to the aspect of selling. Your actual book is critical for future sales, the better you wrote, the more your reader liked it – the more they will buy your books in the future.

BUT; for the first time buyer, your cover page is all you have. It has to look interesting. It has to shout out what your book is about.

The title and Author name has to be BIG and prominent. Keep in mind people will only see a small thumbnail of maybe 15x20 mm – and you have less than 1 seconds to catch their interest.

It is usually good to outsource this to more professional people. See my 'eBook guide' for many links and information about this.

You can use any kind of graphics software to design your front page. For this exercise, I will use another free online designer. Keep it simple and fast. Here we go.

Go to www.canva.com - register and log in with your Google Account, Next select PERSONAL. Look at the short presentation and some samples on the left side.

Pick a background – I used Black colour. Then add an image, I just used one from their online gallery (Elements > Free Photos) – a man standing at a lake with camera in hand. Then pick your text and layout. I did this original front page in about two minutes. Save the image to your computer.

I am sorry to say, you have done it.

This is the End.

Your dream should be ready for publication!

Chapter 7 – After Writing.

It is Wednesday 15 June 2016 and now 05h39. I do not have much free time today – dentist appointment at 11h00 and need to do some shopping. However, from now until about 09h00 I will be able to do my second round of editing on this book. In addition, I am go to copy and write the procedures of getting your book on line.

I am working on three more books in this series, soon to be alive. The first is 'Sell Your Dreams ~ Effective Book Marketing" where I will explain more detail on how to get your book in the best categories and picking the best keywords. The third book is a lot more details about financials and banking, especially for people outside of the USA. In the fourth book, I will be explaining how to generate ideas for stories and/or non-fiction research for quick publishing.

PayPal – If you do not have a PayPal account yet, then now is the time to open that. It is all free. There is lots of information around about PayPal. All you need is an e-Mail address and you will need a local bank account to link with.

Website – to make marketing, references etc. much easier, I do suggest you build a web site for your e-books. There are many free sites and there is plenty of free information around on how to create, design and use such website. It does not need to cost you anything. Many places you can create a suitable website, very easy, very free. I suggest you use WordPress. I have a paid hosting service, but still use the free open source WordPress to design my page. There is plenty of help and videos around to get your site up - looking professional.

Facebook – For the first part of marketing, I suggest you to have a Facebook account.

With your first Dream Book ready, eMail, Website, PayPal and Facebook lined up; all is done. Should not take you more than three hours to do all of these, including the time it will need to verify your details.

Now you need to open another document – Google Docs or any editor. This you will use to make a presentation for your book. I usually give this file the name of the book and ending with 'metadata'. Metadata is all the information that will be used by the book store and search engines in relation to your book. You will need this for every book you post on line.

Please do refer to book #2 in this series for more critical details about the MetaData. *"Sell Your Dreams ~ Effective Book Marketing"*

Title of book:

Sub-Title of book:

Name of author:

Short description of book: Usually not more than 100 words.

Long Description of book: Keep this one to the point and interesting. Tell the potential reader what your book is about. Write it in such way they will have a feeling that they need to buy your book. This is your second most important sales point. Sell your story here, but do not tell everything. You can usually write up to 4000 characters.

Categories: You can usually pick two categories. This should be the most detailed and most applicable categories where people will go to look for your book. There is quite a bit of critical issues I cover in the second book of this series.

KeyWords: (aka Tags): These are important for search engines like Google. Use all the important words to describe your book, content and you can use small phrases like 'sell your dream'. Separate each with a coma.

Price of book: It is up to you. For a first few fiction books, under 10,000 words – I would suggest somewhere between US$ 0.99 and US$ 2.99. Then you may need some other personal information.

All of these are done, so when you post your book you can refer to this, and even copy and paste the required information.

As you are uploading your file, you will get some more data, i.e. the actual code / address of your book. Add this to your metadata for that book.

Now, get back into Google Docs, read your Dream Book for the last time through. If you are happy, then you need to download it to your computer. You can probably do the upload direct from your Cloud, but I have not done it - yet. The file needs to be converted for upload. Go to the Menu>File>Download as> and pick Microsoft Word (.docx). Download the file to your computer, probably in the User\download folder. Make sure where it is because you will need to upload it from there. Make sure you have the image file you created for the front page in the same folder, ready for uploading.

Once you have this ready, you go on to post your book. I suggest you to use Amazon.com as a launching platform. There are many booksellers, at least 74 by my last count, that are not too small. I do cover this in more details with eBook Guide. Some distributors / stores have good features in one aspect, other is better with other issues.

The good thing with SmashWords is that they distribute your book to 17 bookshops – and it will cost you nothing. Your royalties are not much less than when you go and distribute your book all by yourself.

You can expand on this. At present Lulu.com has a very special offer – I hope you will support me while it is ongoing. Let me know, with your e-mail address and I can invite you to join Lulu as Author. That will give me a US$10.00 bonus – and – if invited - you will get a free copy of your first printed book. Please? Register there, and publish your book.

Currently Lulu only distribute to four bookstores. Their royalties are paid monthly. Just make sure you not distribute to the same store from both Smashwords and Lulu – for instance. Both will send your book to Amazon.com. Opt out of that on Smashwords if you will use Lulu.

Get your book published on at least Amazon.com. It should take you less than 2 hours to go through the whole process the first time. They have excellent guides and videos. Then wait for them to send you an e-mail to say your book is on-line – it may take a day or two.

In the meantime, the other main book sellers do have excellent video guidance and education – watch them. They cover a lot of ideas and techniques I did not cover in this quick guide. However, nobody does show you the Google Docs option – yet!

Chapter 8 – Marketing.

Well done, by now you have an eMail address, an editor, a graphics design, PayPal, Website, Facebook page, your book is published (and within limits, my free help if you bought this book and/or eBook Guide). Most important you have your first Dream Book on sale.

However, the fight is not over. Here is the bad news. Your book is one amongst some 9 million other books floating around the internet. The good news is, there are potentially 2 billion people that want to pay you for reading your dreams.

You need to present your book to them. Marketing. I have finished the second book in this series – "Sell Your Dreams ~ Effective Book Marketing". Please, see the last page of this book for info and links.

For now, let us start with the obvious.

On Facebook you will probably have your personal page. Post there about your book, link it to your preferred shop for buying like Amazon - but place your books own direct link there.

Secondly, on the right top of your Facebook menu – go there and create a new PAGE. Use this for all your books, or make a new page for each book. Tell your friends, invite people, get to be known. In addition, there are options when you post on your Page for marketing your book. Start with using the "Boost your Post" option. It is not expensive. See more from Facebook about these options.

Now it is still Wednesday 15 June 2016 and the time is 08h10. I did editing this booklet through to the third time now, added in a few images and the Index. There are 7,223 words on 27 pages. Will go to make breakfast then dentist … While waiting there I am going to use my phone to type a short story about that horrible feelings and observations. Remember this is 'My dream'. I am the crazy boss of my dream. However, this dream at the dentist will be a nightmare.

- - - **E N D** - - -

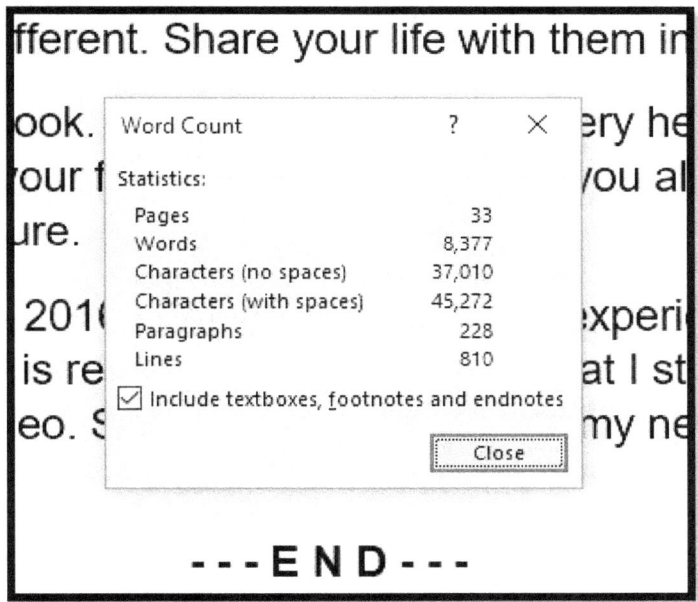

- - - **E N D** - - -

In total I works about 21 hours on this book, 8,377 words, and 33 pages at A5 size – all over a total period of 3 days. I am really surprised.

On Google Docs I dictated 7,473 words on 29 pages in 7.5 hours.

Chapter 9 – The video.

Making and using a video as marketing tool for your book is a great winner. Strangely enough, I do not see many authors doing this effort.

I also made the video (About page 10) as an additional visual guide to this book. Some things are better explained in visual form than words.

I guess one will never reach the point of having your writing perfect. Somewhere you will need to end it and go on to the next one. On the other hand, the more you edit, including the vocal reading back of your text, the better your end product will be. I would say if you read through the whole document, on two different days, and not needed to edit more than one point; then your document is as ready as can be.

For the video recording, I used the build in (Free) Microsoft Screen Capture. If you have an old version of MS-Windows or use a different operating system, there are other good screen capture software. I can recommend "CamStudio" and/or "APowersoft Free Screen Recorder". Search on Google, both are good, though I personally like Microsoft just a little more; except for a 10 minute recording time limit. That is not a problem for this kind of recordings anyway.

For editing; Cut and paste, snip and join and making a bit better, I usually use my favourite PowerDirector and/or DaVinci Resolve (Free). However, both of them has quite a steep learning curve. A fairly good program is the free Microsoft Movie Maker included with Windows.

The video is about 13 minutes long and took me nearly 7 hours to complete. You can view the video on my website.

Chapter 10 - Back Pages.

Usually introduce yourself: As example:

<u>About the Author:</u>

I was born in the Old South Africa, a very long time ago. Yet, for me it feels like yesterday. My life was filled with so many experiences, I will need a whole new life to write about it all. Just so sad that I only discovered this ability at the ripe old age of 59 years.

In South Africa I still have two daughters that are rather happy to stay there. Fortunately my two sons are out, also now working and living near me in Thailand.

Since I was 38 years old, I left from South Africa and the world became my Homeland. I was mining for gemstones in Zambia, cut the gems and made jewellery in Bangkok. Had a hopping around Saudi Arabia, an exploration expedition throughout Somaliland and Djibouti, sometime in Dubai and Jordan before I came back to the East.

In Thailand I started a new venture with building boats, which became a large success. Bakri Cono is today one of the most prestigious Yacht builders in Asia. A scuba diving resort in Lembeh, Indonesia – which we sold when my son became a father. My oldest son took the Chandlery aspect and run with it, today one of the biggest in SE Asia with the very nice name of ASAP-Marine. Yes, ‘*As Soon As Possible*’. The younger one is running the Yacht factory.

As for me, I am now just spending the biggest portion of my time on research and writing.

I really like writing!

Another good idea is to ask for Reviews from your reader.

~ 120 ~

About this book.

To get your book sold, you need people to find it. If you have the best book in the world, but nobody knows about it – you will sell nothing. In the eBook world you are competing against more than 5 million other books. Therefore, you do need to do something that will make your book more 'discoverable'.

This book is about that – to get higher ranking on the sales list, promote it, inform people and generate income for your Dream.

The largest section of this book is about the most important issue for any On-Line type of business – especially eBooks. KEYWORDS. Take a look at the INDEX to see what this book offers.

Allow me to share a trend with you. When people look for Fiction books, they need to use Categories, that way they can find the kind of book they want. On the other hand, using Categories in Non-Fiction is also good, but the potential buyer needs to scroll a long time to find their required book. Since they know exactly what they are looking for in Non-Fiction, it is more effective to search for Keywords. Therefore Keywords are critical.

This is the second book in the "*Sell Your Dream*" series. The first eBook is about how to produce an eBook of more than 5,000 words in less than 24 –working hours. It is also available from the same store where you bought this book. Alternatively you can refer to the author's website.

Introduction.

<u>An early note:</u> In this book I will try not referring to any publisher or store by name. I was hammered on that issue with two of my earlier books. If you do go to my website, there is a list of some of the bigger stores in the world and a little write up about the ones I am using myself. For the sake of this presentation, I will be using the data from the biggest eBook store in the world. Without mentioning their name, I am sure you know who I am referring to.

To be very honest, I have looked at many books, I made an intensive study about what people actually do to get their books sold. After all, I am first a Writer myself, then I like to help people achieve their dreams. I have watched hundreds of videos, paid for two highly selected on-line courses – and did lots of my own research.

Am I right? Well, let us look at the results in a week or so. For now, I am writing this book to explain what I did and how I did it. I will also explain other ideas and concepts, recommended by others, not tried by myself – yet. If you see this book, it means I have achieved some success. If I do not get good results, you would not be reading this book, and I keep on learning.

There are two ways in which people look for books on line. They go to the store and follow links to the Directory or Genre they wish to buy a book. The other one is to go to the store (or sometimes just use a Search Engine like Google) to look for a book according to specific keywords.

These are the four most important things you need to understand, in order of importance: The keywords, proper directory listing, cover page of book and the content of the book.

Everything else is way down the list of importance – if you really want to sell a lot of books.

<u>One issue to define:</u> Marketing is not sales and Sales is not Marketing. They are like the mamma and papa of a baby. Without either there will be no lovely baby. The marketing person usually like to give things away – for free. The sales person usually thinks that is seriously stupid. Sales works in minutes, marketing works for months or years. This book is about Marketing. But, it is also about Sales.

There are people that write, because they love writing. I am definitely in this category. Then there are the people that write as a business. Often they have hundreds of books under their name, but seldom actually wrote it themselves.

There are two ways of writing. From the heart – you write what you feel, that which is on your heart. In my humble opinion, that is the way it should be. The commercial 'writer' seldom fall in this class. When it comes to fiction, I think it is the best way with which to make a real success.

The other way is to write what makes money. Off course, some form of a personal interest is also good here; however it is purely about publishing in large quantity.

As for the purpose of this book; it is valid for both. To successfully publish and sell your book, you need to have the best options for listing and the best keywords. However, the sequence to using this book is then just a little twisted around.

Where the heart writer will finish his book and then find the most suitable niche and keywords, the commercial writer will first find the niche with keywords and then write accordingly. In both cases, the same procedures in this book remains valid.

Besides these descriptions, when you finished working through this book, I would advise you to do more in depth study with regards to Keywords and the operations of Search Engines. Google has quite a lot of documents about that subject.

If you understand and apply the content of this book, you will definitely see happy results in the sales of your books.

The Book Inside.

The actual content you wish to sell. I have seen really crappy books – yet they rate high in the Book lists. You need the content, and that can be anything. However, if the contend is poor quality and of low value, the book might be 'returned'. You lose the income and more important, a future customer. On the other hand, if your content is value for money, the buyer will probably look up on your other published books, and buy future books that you release.

I am not going to spend much time about the content of your book here. Later I will write another book and probably make a video about how to create the content of your book, especially in non-fiction.

There is only one point I would like to stress here. In most book stores the potential buyer gets the option of pre-view the first number of pages. Sometimes you can select like 5% or 10% (Standard). This means you have a potential buyer. ALL the work you did and all the rest of this book is to get the potential customer this far. Do not waste those efforts and your time. Make sure you get the full attention of the customer in those first few pages. The better you can grab the attention of this person, the more likely you will close the sale.

Do not tell your whole story, not even all the key-notes. Create a level of tension, suspension, expectations. Get the reader to desire your book. Period.

I usually have an 'Introduction' – that is my catcher. That is usually right after the Title Page, before the Index. Which brings me to the Index. It is important, do not just make 'Chapter 1' and 'Chapter 2' …. Boring. It is part of your bait! Capture the reader, even with your Index or Content or whatever you might call it.

Look again at the one in this book. There are Chapters, but each has a description. Try to make it interesting, short Keyword like. That will tell the customer what he can expect in the book. Yes, even in your fiction Dream Story.

Tommy write his fiction book and he has Chapters 1 to 8. Ok, there are breaks.

You come and you write the same story, but your Chapters might look like this:
Chapter 1 – Breakdown.
Chapter 2 – Smoking Gun.
Chapter 3 – Trapped.
Chapter 4 – Shipwrecked. … And so on. Whose book is the more likely one to be sold?

The bottom line is: Keep the beginning (and hopefully all of your book) interesting, captivating and worthwhile to read. Give the customer what he/she wish for. There is an interesting sales slogan:

"Sell Dreams, not Products".

Steve Jobs of Apple once said *"You have to accommodate what people dream of, produce the product they want and sell it to them. Giving them the satisfaction of buying something they dreamt of."*

Make a dent in the universe

- Do not be afraid of getting things wrong
- Do not limit yourself.
- Do what most people will not do
- Learn to be ok with who you are and where you are
- Do something that will change people life.

The Cover Page.

Yes, some people claim this to be the most important. It is important, but not the most important. A good cover page will grab the attention of the potential buyer. However, if your book is listed somewhere far down in the search list, like page 72 – even the best of cover pages will not help you anything at all.

Your cover page needs to shout, the louder the better. Read – *'To be Different'*. There is absolutely no value in a very complicated dense graphics cover page. Keep it simple. A big difference from the bookshop cover page is the size. Mostly people will see your book's front page in something like 2x3 cm size.

A clean looking easy background image. Not too much clustered in colours and objects. Then you add the Title of your book, Sub-Title and your name. Done. Clean, simple, easy, and fast.

this is a bad font.

This is a good font.

Do make sure your title is an easy to read font. Remember, you have a time restriction to overcome. The difference between a bad text font and a good font on the cover page will make or break your books sale. Most people do not actually 'read' the characters of a word; they pick the 'image' of that word. To put it in another way, here is a word 'read' – did you read it as 'r – e – a – d = read' or did you immediately see 'read'?

Keep the title on top or left-top. First to read as normal eye movement across a page. If it is a complicated font, the reader's mind might not capture the meaning other than 'something'. Follow that up with a sub-title, also easy to read but less critical.

In the eBook store, you have between half a second and one second time to capture the potential buyer. Once skipped over your Cover image, they are goners. You can use anything you like, but I will suggest the following:

It might be a good idea to source your cover image out. I do not know, maybe. However, you can rather spend the money on a good cup of coffee – unless you do not know how to use any graphics program. Follow these simple rules and you will be OK. As example I took six cover pages. There are some graphics designs that comes into play, to a certain extend. Things like matching colour templates, sizes of words, etc. Though in a 2x3 cm thumbnail it does not really matter so very much anymore. The actual Title is more important.

Preferably, use a background image that conveys the message of your book. Use contracting colour(s) for the text like title and author, but not more than two colours.

See in the following image what I mean about good and very good cover pages. These are my humble opinion, you are welcome to follow your own heart. Initially I also went for the more colourful, jammed up, clutter pages where I want the page to tell the whole story. I quickly realized that was a big mistake.

There is also a little trick you can play, although it is not always effective since books cover pages gets re-arranged. If all the books are in brilliant colours, you place a black-and-white. That will stand out, as is the top left image.

As a rule, the colours yellow to orange generally draws the eye. See this image below. But, it is not a good colour to use on all types of books. Every colour has the tendency to generate an 'emotion'.

Yellowish are warnings. Green and blue are more calming, violet generates a feeling of spirituality, red is hot, blue is cold, etc.

	Is it the Books name, or the Author? What is the message of the book?		Name difficult to read. Lose time, loose eye. Background tells nothing.
	Very difficult to read title or author. The background is OK.		This looks like a 'professional', but; name takes time, image has no message. Customer lost.
	This, IMHO is a very good page. Perfect to see the message in the image and all the texts.		Clutter, confusion, psychotic. Maybe this is the story?

The only other thing you do need to know is that all keywords in the Title and sub-title must be capitalized; the same with the first and last words. By capitalize, I mean first letter only. To write the whole word in uppercase is bad. A good way to please everyone is to capitalize all words, and/or just leave the binding words like a, them, and, etc. as small first letters.

To review, a good clean background, easy to read fonts and only the title, sub-title and authors name (in contrasting colours) makes the best book covers.

The next two chapters re running hand in hand. Both are more important than the Cover Page.

Tip: You can always change the Cover Page Images. Some sites demands that the Title, Sub-Title and Authors name on the cover page must match the data file for the book exactly.

The Art of Keywords.

Suck your thumb, a few nice words may be popping out. But, that is not the effective way to do. Keywords are for your book as important as the key for a locked safe door. There are good keywords, there are bad words. However, this is a true form of art. Or maybe it is a simple matter of understanding.

There are two arguments when it comes to keywords, and these are the first points you need to consider. Do you want to use a word that has millions of searches per day, or do you want a word that has only a hundred searches per day. It is up to you.

For a long time I followed the second option, believing that if I have more complicated keywords with less resulting links, then better for me. But, it does not work that way. At least not when you are looking for business.

The big question is not what you think, but rather what the potential buyer will use as he is searching for a book. If the target buyer of your book is highly educated person, then a keyword like 'Phrontistery' will place you in a position with virtually no competition. However how many people will use phrontistery? The common mass market will rather refer to 'place of study', 'school' or 'university'.

Therefore, it is much better to use common high level keywords that does indeed yield millions of pages. BUT, then you must understand the system – and ride it like a wild horse.

THIS, my dear reader, is the second most critically important aspect of selling your book. The right SET of keywords.

It is not only used by people searching for a book in the Category we explained in the next chapter - but it directs people towards your book from way out there; long before they get to the book dealer. Even before they might be thinking of buying a book. All search engines, like Google, Bing, Yahoo, etc. make extensive use of keywords. If you can master the 'Art of Keywords', not only will it help you in research, but it will be your best marketing tool.

Think of anything you wish, condense it to one single word, the most applicable – and you have a Keyword. Because there are only so many words in any language, and searching trillions of documents to find a single keyword will result in one unbelievable useless list.

The most used on-line word in the English language was 'sex'. Presently, in Google it yields 644+ Million results in 0.72 seconds. Now, if I define my search more and say I am looking for 'ancient sex' then I get 50 million results. Make it even better and search 'ancient Mongolian sex' there are 664,000 results. Define more, 'ancient Mongolian juvenile sex' yields 78,000 results. It is still a hell of a lot, but more manageable. You can usually use up to 5-word phrases effectively.

This is where the magic starts. Many people are selling courses and 'secrets' about the eBook Keyword. Some are good, most are junk. I will give you everything in this book, almost for free. You do not need to buy a US$199.00 course to learn what is for free anyway. Listen to me, <u>THERE IS NO SECRET</u>. Just pure understanding and logic. That is all.

I can give you a nice list of the best keywords, but that might do you no good. In addition, the market for strong keywords are fluctuating; it changes on a whim. Twenty years ago, one of the best searching keywords were 'sex' but today it is surpassed by 'Sale' with twice as many returns.

A year ago the word 'BREXIT' would have very little results. On 23 June 2016 there were 122 million, on 27 June 2016 were 147 million results from Google. Today, 30 June 2016, there are 181+ million listed links to BREXIT.

Therefore, rather than tell you the best hundred keywords, I will show you how to find the better options for keywords by yourself.

What is your book about? Get it defined into one single keyword. First most important point – is that keyword in your Title? If you are writing fiction, it is not so critical. If you are writing Non-Fiction and that keyword is not in your Title or Sub-Title - then I suggest you either change the keyword, or you edit the titles.

Using BREXIT as search keyword in our not-named bookshop, at the moment there is a list of 106 books. On the first page, 11 out of 16 listing has the word BREXIT within the first two words of their main title. None of the remaining books has the word BREXIT amongst the first three words of their title. In 53 other books the word does appear towards the end of a long title *(one title has BREXIT as the 11th word in a 16 word title)* or in the sub-titles. The remaining ones probably have the word in their keyword list but not in either title or sub-title.

Tip: A particular powerful keyword in the title is at least ten times more important than that same keyword in the keywords list.

Next you expand your list of keywords to something like 30 words and short phrases in total. You will thin them out to minimum 7 and maximum 15. Do keep in mind variations and synonyms of a word. For example 'dream, dreams, dreamed, dreaming' are all different keywords. The same you find 'neighbour (67 mil) and 'neighbor' (141 mil) yields different results. You can play with words like 'take-out' or 'take out' or 'take away' – all correct, depending on what the reader is searching.

On this point there is also another critical point to keep in mind.

Geography. Consider your potential reader. If he is a bit more educated he will type 'television' rather than 'telly' or 'tube'. Basically, if your book is more British Isles targeted, then use British keywords. As example the American say 'counter-clockwise' vs the British 'Anti-clockwise'. Or biscuit vs cookie. A block of flats vs apartment building. There are a few websites where you will get comprehensive lists. (Try for instance www.englishclub.com).

<u>Tip:</u> Try to remain with words that are generally the same in all regions and not often misspelled.

Next, with your highly selected list of keywords, you go to see what it gives you when you use it to do a search.

For the following examples I will be referring to – and use, and do the same time – my eBook "Sell Your Dreams". Obviously my main keyword is 'Dreams'; secondary is 'Sell'; and as third 'Marketing'.

Yes, I know this sounds complicated and it is quite a bit of work. BUT. If you do this right, that means you are done for some time, your eBook will keep on making money for times to come – without your input.

Opened Google and type 'Dreams' – 293 million results. 'Sell' has 674 million results and 'Marketing' yields a staggering 1.12 billion results. What that tells you is that each keyword is a top-rate keyword, it is something people search for every day, many times. That means, your keywords will get 'shown' a lot. Not that it will result in sales – yet.

Make good use of the Google Suggest option in the search bar. While typing Google tends to suggest or predicts your word. That is an auto feature that is already very helpful. Try to type the word 'neighbour'. By the time you typed 'n...' google already give you a possible list of words, so the list keeps updating until you press the Search. That also gives you possible keywords you might use. Notice in this case the listing of Neighbor is before Neighbour – it is simply because I did a search for that particular word before – and because the first listed word is used more often than the next one.

Try to play with a few words, maybe 'pancake…'.

As example, I used the English word 'fylfot' which yields 99,900 results against 'swastika' that has 8.07 million results – both means the same thing, yet one word is less know. In this case you will rather use 'swastika' than 'fylfot'.

I have one acronym 'Habega' which yields only 5,800 results; that means very few people knows it. Maybe one would think it is easier to be spotted, but consider the big picture. If only 100 people will search for your keyword, very few of them might even be interested in a book.

Now back to the main search line. Let us see what we get by combining the two words. If I enter 'sell' and 'dream' I get 71 million results. If I place the two words in quote marks, 'sell dreams' I get only 30,100. Now we have two strong words and they narrow down nicely. Let us see what happens when we add 'sell' and 'dreams' and 'marketing'. As loose words we get 500,000 sites. That is not bad. Now if we place them in quotes "sell dreams marketing" we get only 6 results. The semi-quote means all words in order but not necessary as phrase. Double quote means in order and as exact phrase.

Your target is to go through this method and expand or delete words from your list. Look for words that are used often. In the above case of 'fylfot'; unless it has a very particular reason to use that less-known word; I would rather swop it out for the 'swastika' synonym.

We are not finished yet. All that we know now is that we do have some powerful, often used, keywords. Let us look again back, word for word what Google says, using 'sell'.

Sell, 675 million links listed. Now scroll down on that page. First you will find some synonyms or more descriptive words. See if there are some interesting words you might use as keywords. In my case, nothing really very usable.

Then further down to the bottom of the page, there you will find a section "Searches Related to ….'. In this case, there is no usable alternatives applicable for me either.

Searches related to sell	
sell **vs sale**	sell **any car**
difference between sale and sell	**quick** sell
sell **verb**	**cross** sell
sell **me**	**car** sell

The next word 'Dreams' also did not have any usable alternatives. The same with 'Marketing'. Then I join 'Sell Dreams' – which gave some interesting readings, but no usable alternatives for keywords.

The bottom line is that for Google we have three powerful keywords.

Now let us get back to our eBook keywords. **The first place to** search is off course right there where you are going to post your book. For most of the eBook Stores, you need a separate login for buyer or author. In this case I just went to www.,,,,.com and there, second line from the top is a search box. On the left side there is a selection drop-down menu, at first set for 'All'. I opened the selection and picked 'Books'. Then, in the Search box, I type 'Dreams' – immediately a Suggestion box opens up to help me refine my search. This is what it looks like.

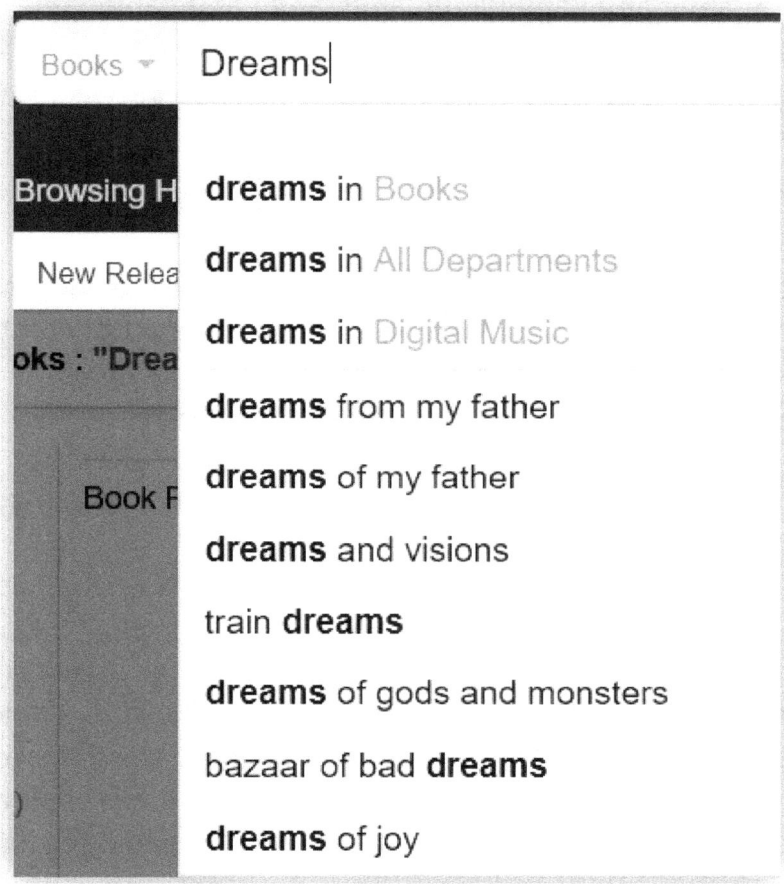

Right there, while you are typing, is your first clue for searching results. We can call it Prime Keywords. These are actual phrases people use when they were searching about the main keyword(s) you are just typing in.

Since none is perfect fitting phrase for my book, I picked 'Dreams in Books' next. That means it will open the Books section and show me titles which has the word '… dreams …' embedded. There were 738,148 results. A lot of competition. Since my book is only in eBook format, I picked on the eBook list. The numbers are down to 50,969.

Keep in mind, this first book was just published two weeks before I am collecting this information.

Sorting by 'Relevance' I found my book on Page #3, about the 51st in the whole list. Not too bad, BUT it is also in part due to the build in promotional algorithms that give some advantage for new books. No star rating, no reviews.

Next there is a bit of a cheat. I did not realise this before, but this can be used to boost your sales. When I select to sort by "Publication Date" it is listed in order of dates published. That is where you find another feature. Some books are on Pre-Order. The highest ranking book is listed to publish on 30 December 2030. Stupid. BUT... when I click on the book, it is already available for sale, as Pre-Order. It is supposed to be available for up to 90 days before the release of the book. Now, the good to use this is that you can list your book, and get sales. If people look for publish by date, this will automatically give you and higher page listing than any book already available. Do note, your book will not be delivered and you will not be paid for the sale until the book's actual delivery date. I found my book on Page 20. There were 13 books published on the same day.

There are other 'Sorts by...' which I will not cover now, after all it is a new book. No Reviews yet –and not for free, neither too expensive.

Let us move on one step. Now I will search in the applicable category. So in this case I know the book is currently listed under category 'Non-Fiction' > 'Self Help' (123,515 books). So going there and then type 'Dreams", I get a listing of 3,525 with my book #5 sorted as 'relevance'. That is a very good place to be, but I will have to work in keeping it there i.e. reviews and ratings.

The two keywords sell and dreams – give me a first book listing. Considering that these two words are often used power keywords, and they do give me a first page listing – I am very happy with them.

Now let us expand a bit to search phrases. In the self-publishing geek lingo it is referred to as 'Long tail Keywords'. This is how to find out what other people are using when they do a search with your related keywords.

Tip: Use the most suitable power keywords first and go down the list in order of importance.

In some bookstores they only allow seven keywords. Other stores allows up to 500 characters. One important thing to keep in mind here. IF you are using the Distribution services of some preferred company that allows you a lot of keywords, and you opt in for them to distribute your book to for instance Amazon with only seven keywords – they will and can only use the first seven keywords from their list. Thus, make sure your most important keywords are listed first.

In addition, the title and sub-title of your book do carry more weight in Search engine results than the keyword metadata. Most on-line eBook stores accept up to 250 characters in the Title and another 250 in the Sub-Title. However, keep it as short as possible. See the Cover Page Chapter. Do not use the title or sub-title in your keywords, unless you have way enough space for what you need.

Every word in the Title and Sub-Titles are already recognised as a keyword by the search engines. There is no value in duplicate keywords. Rather use other power-keywords, in the keyword list, to expand the discoverability of your book.

How to expand on your keywords, besides the single word that describe your book and your title? Think about the topics, themes, geographical settings and period in your book and start making a list of the possibilities. Then you go back to Google and see which are the more powerful words or alternatives.

A good target for your listing of keywords, within your book genre is between 100 and 1,000 items. Less than 100 indicates not many people use those keywords – or if the keywords are strong, you have hit right on a gold mine. If it is more than 1,000 you should consider other keywords, the competition will be too tuff.

Tip 1: A good keyword is one that has a very high number of listings in google or your eBook store. The best secondary keywords must also have a high number of listing, but they would preferably have a reduction in total number of links when used as short phrase with the main keyword.

Tip 2: Change your keywords from time to time. There is absolute NO restriction on you changing the keywords for your book posting anywhere. This is a great truth, which distributors does not do and very few authors knows about. When a book's sales are dropping, go and change your keywords! This is especially useful on sites where you are very restricted with your keywords.

Tip 3: Use a Thesaurus (Or google Similar" for finding related and / or similar keywords.

Advanced Key Wording.

Keywords Everywhere:

Besides the hard labour methods, there are also other options available to assist you with keyword searches. Some are free; some are limited free and other cost money. One option that is 'free' on condition is the Google Add Words.

Until mid-2015, it was a very open, free keyword planner, but since it is more restricted to setting up your Google Add Words campaigns. Thus, at minimum you need to supply Credit Card Info. It is a handy tool.

Personally I think a good basic understanding, as I explained above, combined with a Thesaurus should be more than perfect. This is one reason, although the same reason is against and in favour of my suggested methods.

When you are using the Keyword Software or Apps, you become limited to their search algorithm. These are quite good, BUT people change dynamically and people search different. The computer robots can only look for how many times a word has been searched for, regardless the reason, results or personal requirements of the searcher. In example, the name of this series of books is "Sell Your Dreams". The first keyword is 'Sell" with a staggering 1.5 billion results. 'Your' is not really a keyword, though as word it does yield 18 trillion results. The keyword 'Dreams' is a very powerful keyword with over 7 million results. How many of those are from people looking to buy a book?

String them together in a long-tail keyword of three words "Sell Your Dreams" – now I have 422,000 results. Add the search operator +book and we are down to 1,030. Change the search factor to +eBook and we remain with only 145 results. In

Google, it gives at least 14 links to my books within the first 10 pages. Interesting enough, none of those is to Amazon.com; but seven are to my own website and Facebook, two links to Smashwords.com.

First, there is another very helpful app I suggest you add to your Google Chrome. It is 'Keywords Everywhere'. Go to Google Chrome Web Store and search "Keywords Everywhere". Select and install the App to your Google Browser. The App logo is a Black Circle with a red 'K' in it.

The first advantage this tool has, it is giving you immediate information about the subject you are searching for in Google. An indicator (Google data extract) of how many searches your keyword or phrase has per month and the average CPC (Cost per Click) value in Google Add Sense.

From this result on Gambia we can see there is an average of about 165,000 searches with that keyword per month and the cost value is at US$0.60 per click. Your target is to get the highest values for both these two numbers when you are looking for keywords.

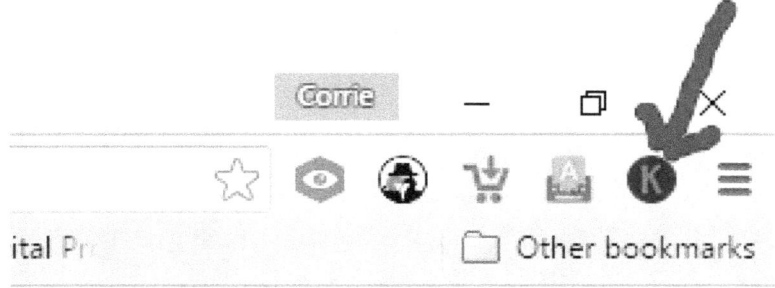

Next, you can click on the Keyword Icon (Right top bar of your Google Chrome) and have a page open where you can type in a group of keywords, separated by commas.

There is a button 'Setting' where you can change some options, i.e. Global or USA or AU alone, the currency you use and then from where the data is to be collected. There are currently 11 optional sources, including Uber-Suggest which is our next tool.

Searching that will give you a table with the monthly search volume per word and its CPC value. Click on the titles to sort your results i.e. Search Volume to sort in numerical order.

You can export this to a spreadsheet (MS-Excel or Google Sheet) for further manipulations.

Show 50 ▼ entries

Copy | Excel | CSV | PDF | Print

Search:

Keyword	Search Volume	CPC
gambia	165,000	$0.60
political	40,500	$1.29
riot	201,000	$1.33
tourism	74,000	$1.05
economy	135,000	$1.62

Showing 1 to 5 of 5 entries

Previous | 1 | Next

UberSuggest: (http://www.ubersuggest.io)

Maybe one should use 'UberSuggest' before 'Keywords Everywhere'. Maybe not – it is up to you to develop your own strategy. Anyway, these two Apps resonate together. They are a very powerful tool to use in your keyword searching, better than any commercial package I had a look at.

When you have your basic keywords, you enter then one by one into UberSelect, or the keyword Phrase if you so wish. UberSelect will then give you a very long list of additional keywords that is found in searches, linked with your keyword, before and/or after. These you can then select from, copy and run them all through Keywords Everywhere again.

Google Trends: https://www.google.com/trends/

After we worked through all of the above options and we have a number of good keywords and long-tail-keywords, finally we need to run them through Google to see how they are performing – in history and at present. There is a company that can do all of this for you – they charge around US$ 88 per month subscription.

The nice of Google Trends is that you can see how people are searching over the history of a few years, and currently, you can see the demographic searches for this keyword. Here you will be surprised to find how a particular keyword yields results. There is a table for related searches.

Because our keywords here (Gambia) are very low ranking, I used two other current high trend keywords – just to show the powers of Google Trends. I compared Donald Trump with Hilary Clinton.

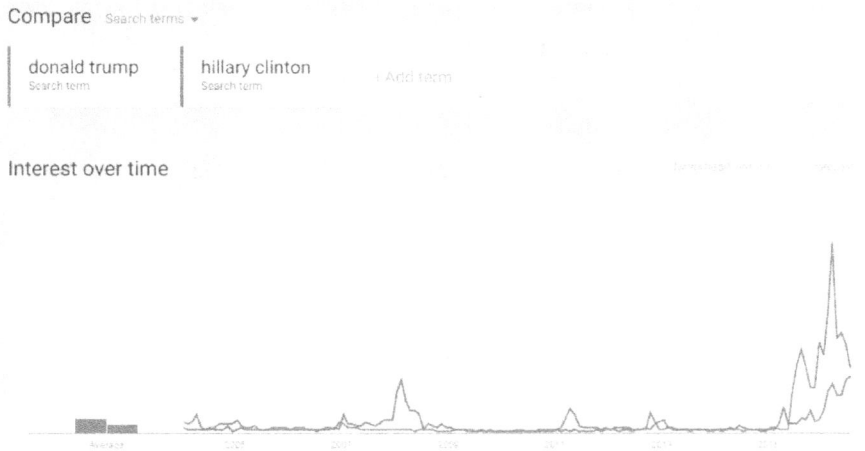

We can see how Clinton got surged – Around end of 2008 when she stood against Obama and again at present for the Presidential election. Donald Trump had a great spike since beginning of 2016 with his Presidential campaign. When on the graph, you can move your mouse over the lines to see the scale of interest.

If you then have a keyword that is spiking at present, it is good. If you have a keyword that has always an interest, that is better on the long term.

The next graph is Geopolitical. It shows the index of searches per country in the world, listing the higher rated ones on the right. Again, you can move your mouse over the map and see the index for each country. In this case, very interesting, we see the Index for this Trump / Clinton search from Russia and China is actually 0. Vietnam is 7, Japan is one.

So how to use this for your book? I wanted to write a book about President Paul Kruger of South Africa. I find a History index of nearly 1 and regional 7 from South Africa. It is not going to be a good selling book, the interest is very low. Now, if you are writing a book about Clinton and Trump, such has a good interest from ten countries. However, if your target market is Russia or China, there will be very little sales.

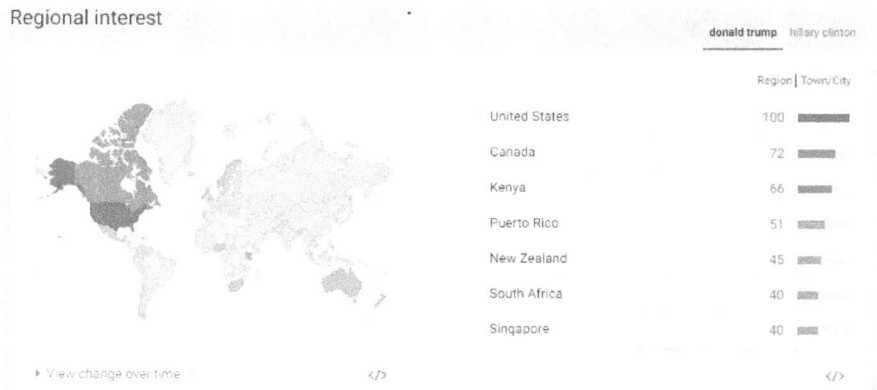

The next graph has a few options. Basically you see this:

donald trump **hillary clinton**

Topics	Top	Rising	Queries	Top	Rising
Hillary Rodham Clinton - Former U.	100		benghazi		Breakout
Donald Trump - Businessman	5		bernie sanders		Breakout
Bernie Sanders - United States Se.	5		donald trump		Breakout
Bill Clinton - 42nd U.S. President	5		hillary clinton 2016		Breakout
2012 Benghazi attack - Disaster	0		sanders		Breakout
Democratic Party - Political party	0		trump		Breakout
Ted Cruz - United States Senator	0		barack obama		+800%

Do note there are two options in each of the result indexes. The 'Top rated' and the 'Rising.' In the particular case we find in both columns, with the Rising option – there are a lot of 'Breakouts' which means the current interest is rising very rapidly.

At the same time, you can see more options for long-keywords.

Google Keyword Planner.

This is an excellent keyword tool – but it is part of the Google AdWords campaigns. Once upon a time, just a few months ago this was an open easy to use tool. Now you need to register for AdWords and open a new campaign in order to use this feature. Whichever way, I think Keywords Everywhere is an easier to use tool – for the present.

The Category.

Depending on your country, synonyms used for same purpose are Niche, Genre or Directory. Mostly you will find these four words used in the same context. However, for the purpose of this book I am going to use the little bit finer definition.

Before we go on, let us assume I just finished a book. This book is a non-fiction history of the Inuit people of Northern America and I call my book draft "People on Ice".

Directory or Category: This is the main division of books into various type. As example: Fiction or Non-fiction; which could be divided into listings like Romance, Crime, Sci-Fi, History, Engineering, etc.

Niche: Is the sub-directory, usually down to the last set of listings. As example (using my imaginary book above): From the main Non-Fiction Category list there is a sub-Category – 'History'. From there another sub-sub-Directory 'Americas' and a sub…sub of 'Canada' and finally under Canada we get 'First nations', which does not have any more sub-divisions. Normally we will write this as Non-Fiction > History > Americas > Canada > First Nations. (In some cases people use a ' : ' in place of the ' > ' which is the same meaning. Anyway, the 'First Nations' is the end of the line – that is a Niche.

Genre: is basically referring to both or either Directory and Niche.

All the bigger eBook stores has a list of genre. That is to help people find the exact book they are looking for. In the physical bookstore, this is the 'Section' where you will find the kind of book you want. The eBook store is the same as a normal book shop – the more books they have, the more Sections (Categories) they apply to enable the buyer finding the book they want easier. Usually there are two main Categories. Fiction and Non-Fiction.

Fiction is stories, not based on real incidents. Typically it might be mystery, suspense, romance, drama, etc. Non-fiction is everything that is based on the real. It could be history, engineering, diet, religion, etc.

If you list your beautiful Romantic story under Non-Fiction > Engineering, it will not sell anything. The same if you list your 'Bible Study' book with marvellous discoveries and pictures under 'Fiction > Erotica' it is unlikely you will even sell one book.

Here is an example of a really poor listing. How can a book be True and Not-True (Fiction and Non-Fiction). Maybe a bit far-fetched one can argue about History and Adventure as sub-categories. But then when you go to the Tags (Which is Keywords) – I fail to see the relevance of Tourism, business and economy in this book. Frankly, it is a very confusing listing. To use 'Thailand eBook' is purely a waste of resources. It is a pity this author did not read this book – yet. He would have done so much better with all the books he has listed. He is an author with excellent historical books.

Nonfiction » History » Asian » Asia / Southeast Asia
Fiction » Adventure » General
Published by ▮▮▮▮▮▮▮▮▮▮▮▮
Published: June 25, 2016
Words: 69,150
Language: English
ISBN: ▮▮▮▮▮▮▮▮▮
Tags: thailand travel guide | thailand tourism | thailand culture | thailand business information | thailand ebook | thailand economy | thailand history book

An out-of-category book will lose at least half of its potential sales. Wrong keywords will lose 45% of the potential sales. People who search by category are more likely to buy your book because they know exactly what they are looking for. The keyword searcher might still be floating around. The best option: Right keywords, Right category. Everything else fades away.

Normally the big eBook stores allows you to list your book in two Categories (Some allow only one, others allow more). Use it, and use it wisely. List your book in as many categories you possibly can, but do keep it related to the content of your book. If you have a nice 'Healthy Herbal Diet' book, you can for instance list it under different niches like Cooking, Health, Diet, Weight loss, Herbs, etc.

In this case, first you go to the most likely Categories, follow the options down to the best suited Niche and list your book there.

Then you do the same with every other applicable Category, as many as you can.

Tip: You don't need to always follow the list and sub-lists to the end. If you reach a Sub-Category with less than say 2,000 books – that is good enough. Yes, in practice, you can go lower down. The less books there are, the less opposition you have. But the opposite is also valid; the less books there are, the less people search that far down. Rather use Keywords to get your lower niches.

The categories (genres) you have chosen are crucial and need to be as narrowly focused as possible. Next, when you add the keywords, you can use the keywords of some other related categories or niches.

Let us look back at our imaginary book example earlier. When we look at the sub-category of eBooks > History there are 428,633 books. That is way too many to compete with. Thus narrow it to 'Americas' (68,302 books) which is still too many. Let's look at 'Canada' – There we have only 3,080 books. Now, here we have a very good category. The number is not too small to be obscure, neither too big for strong competition.

We have two options, go further down to the final Niches – all are excellent. When we look at the final (Niches) under 'Canada', we find for instance First Nations (312), Canada (445), Pre-Confederation (418), Province & Local (210). Very small number to compete with, but they also indicate not many people looking there.

The good option we have is to place your book under 'Canada' and then add keywords (You can add seven keywords here, more on other sites) – 'First Nations' and 'Canada'. Effectively your book is now listed in three 'niches' – and you still have one Category with five keywords left to play with.

Now it is time to get back to look at the Title and Sub-Titles of our book. "People on Ice".

"People on Ice" could mean so many things. It could be about arctic explorers or Ice-Hockey, or ski in the Alps. The title might be too broad. Maybe I should consider changing the Title?

Look at our first set of Niches – we have great keyword options there. 'First Nations' sounds like a perfect key-phrase to consider. How about 'Canada'? Or 'North-America'?

Ok, first let us play with 'North America'. Back to our searches we go eBooks > History (283,000) > Americas (68,000) > Hmmm. Problem. There is not a 'North America' – BUT what I see is 'Native American 3,016)'. Here is a game changer in my mind, so lets us follow that one. 'Native American' is the end of the line – the Niche.

How about changing my Title to "Native Americans of Canada" – now my title is a full set of keywords on its own; AND I already tell the potential reader what the book is about. Further, I have two Genres set with low level of competition.

Before I get to close my Keywords; there is one other powerful point to research. The Sub-Title. It is part of the name of your book, it has great Search results value. Looking at what we know for now, we have the tribal name of the people (Inuit) and we know our book is an ancient history. Since there are no other value to use from the Niches that we have as options, now we can play with the Keywords. On this stage we can maybe say "The Ancient Inuit People".

Title – 'Native Americans of Canada'
Sub Title – 'The Ancient Inuit People'
(Yes, in practice I might change the two Titles round).
Category #1: Non-Fiction > History > Americas > Canada
(3,080 books to compete with).

Category #2: Non-Fiction > History > Americas > Native American (3,056 books to compete with).

Keywords: *First Nations, Ancient Inuit People, North America*, … and we have four places left to fill with other Keywords.

Next we can go back to the main search bar and do a full search with the keywords of our new title "Native, Americans, Canada". How many books are there with the same three keywords in their title? None. That is very good, you want this number to be as low as possible, preferably less than ten – provided you are using powerful keywords.

Have a look at the search results (Titles) for other possible keywords. In this case I notice 'Aboriginal' in the title of another book. That is a very suitable and important word, so add it to the keywords.

Before we close this section off, there is one more issue you will find very helpful. Go to each of the final Niches you selected and take a look at how the book in that niche is fairing on the overall listing of best sellers. This is not always available on all book shops, but Kindle is good with it. Sometimes people are looking for best sellers rather than other criteria.

In Kindle, you go to the detail page of a number of books in the final genre – try something between 10 and 20 of the first listed books, then skip maybe 5 pages and also look there. The more you search, the better perspective you will have. Scroll down and you will see the 'Product Details'. It may look something like the image below.

Tip: I use Google Chrome and have an App added to make things much easier and faster: 'AMZ Seller Browser'. (Web link on my website). This app gives me the Kindle Ranking of the listed books. Very useful.

Low down there is the Ranking of that particular book, in overall of the Book Store and then in each of the categories where the book is listed. Typically you would like to see at least one of the books on the first two pages to have and overall rating of less than 20,000. The lower the better. That will indicate to you there is reasonable interest in that genre. The lower that number, the better the Niche is.

Next you can look at the ratings of the Best seller books within that particular niche, look at their prices, number of pages – and publication dates. You only want to look at best sellers, and books with a price tag. Do not concern with free books, Future date release or reviews.

Those all can be a great help to determine your potential success. This will also help you on later stage to determine your price!

Product Details

File Size: 1638 KB
Print Length: 416 pages
Publisher: HarperCollins e-books; Reprint edition (October 13, 2009)
Publication Date: October 13, 2009
Sold by: Amazon Digital Services LLC
Language: English
ASIN: B000N0WTT2
Text-to-Speech: Enabled
X-Ray: Not Enabled
Word Wise: Enabled
Lending: Not Enabled
Enhanced Typesetting: Not Enabled
Amazon Best Sellers Rank: #88,301 Paid in Kindle Store (See Top 100 Paid in Kindle Store)
   #1 in Kindle Store > Kindle eBooks > History > Americas > Canada > First Nations
   #4 in Books > History > Americas > Canada > First Nations
   #11 in Books > History > Military > Canada

Near the bottom there is a section 'Best Seller Rank'. The further down the listings of books you can go with this 'Best Seller Ranking' while having a best seller listed with ranking less than 20,000 the better. The lower that ranking number is, the better the niche. That means that overall, amongst all 5 million books there are a good number of books from this category that get a large number of sales.

If you see the books on page one of the listing are all ranked with higher than 40,000 in Kindle, get out. Not many people are buying books from that category. The opposite is valid when you get at book #50 and you see they are still ranked with lower numbers than 10,000 – that is a good Niche. BUT, maybe that good niche will be very tuff to compete with.

While looking at the Ranking of a particular book, also take a good look at the other niches where that book is listed. That is a great potential guide for you to investigate. See where else your book might fit, or look at those categories / niches to see the potential listing options.

In review: If you find a good niche with not too much competition in numbers of books, and there is at least one best seller with an overall rating less than 5,000 – then you have a smoking hot niche. Do not tell too many people. Accidental, this exact niche we are looking at here happens to be a hot potential.

Tip 1: Mostly you can change the Title and Sub-title of your book even after publishing. In some stores you are not allowed to change the title – especially when it is ISBN registered. In Amazon they are using an ASIN code (Not ISBN) which is like the 'Personal ID code' for your book. That can't be changed. Do remember (mostly) if you do change the Title and Sub-Title – you also need to change the same on your book's Cover Page.

Tip 2: In time, you can move the book to a different category or niche. People have a particular 'like' in what they want to read and therefore the keywords they use most often are the same. Maybe they search for 'Native Americans' in Mexico, not realising there are also Native American in Canada. Maybe I have a section describing how the people live today, so I can move the book to 'Ethnic and National' with only 578 listings). By slipping your book into another genre, with different keywords – you get a whole new exposure.

Subluminal

Ahh, this is most likely one of the less understood words. I have watched many videos, I wrote a few articles, will probably write another book about this extremely useful tool. As a matter of interest, I already picked a name;

Subluminal Shouting.
~ Understand it, use it – be a winner. ~

At first, while the word 'subluminal' seems to be mystical; in truth it is the opposite. Most, and I mean more than 99%, of everybody talking about 'Subluminal Messages' got the tiger on the tail.

The general concept is that your eyes and brain absorb a lot more information than what most people realize. So you will see an image, while you look at the point of interest, there is also some other messages being transplanted into your mind. This is what is for some reason called 'sub-luminal'. Literally meaning 'under light' or un-noticed. Something your brain sees, absorbs and post somewhere in a grey cell –without you really being aware of that action.

This is one important thing to understand. Subluminal is NOT hidden. It is not something you need to go and search for, it is not nearly invisible. It is rather the contrary. Let us look at a few samples.

Here is a very well-known logo. Can you see the sub-luminal message? I will come back to it later.

This is another one, used often to describe 'sub-luminal'. See the arrow between the last Big E and the x?

And then finally this one. The well-known KFC add. Can you see the little dollar note in the lettuce?

So, zoom nicely out and look at these three logos. Can you see the sub-luminal messages? Oh yea, they are there, but I am sure you missed it. To start explaining this important concept, I first want to show you a photo I took of a street in Cambodia.

I took this photo, unintentionally. Can you see the subluminal message? Look carefully what you see in this image. Once I point it out to you, as always with the above images – it will shout at you. You will never miss it again. See the yellow minibus, the additional loading in the back? Quite interesting, but . . .

Do not tell me you missed it!

Loud and clear there is something that you did see, maybe you do not realise it. It is the big red billboards for 'Cambodia beer'. There is another beer in Cambodia called 'Angkor'. Wherever you go in that amazing country, you will find rows upon rows of these two signs. They shout at you from everywhere.

Now you will realize that you did indeed see, and noticed, them – but you probably did not actually think about them.

That my reader, is the truth about Subluminal messages. Now, go back to the Coca Cola logo above. What is the sub-luminal message? In that little red circle is what many people see as the Danish flag. But it is not the message! The Message is 'Coca Cola'. The same with FedEx. The KFC advert is a typical Hidden message, but it is not subluminal.

To bring all of this back to the subluminal marketing of your book is – Get the name of your book posted. Everywhere. Do not tell people everywhere "Buy my book called Sell your Dreams". Write something of interest, and related to your book. Then just in the passing by you mention the name of your book. That brings us to Social Media.

Subluminal messages does not need to be an image. I played one on you, the reader as example. In this chapter I prompted you already with a message! Yes, I am (not) sorry. I want you to understand this concept and use it. Can you remember the words 'Subluminal Shouting'? It is right there in the very first paragraph. The name of a future book I may write.

A little bit of expanding on the issue of Keywords here. The actual word 'Subluminal' appears 54,000 times in a Google search. Thus, it is not a very strong keyword. However, it is a good keyword to use in case somebody does do research about it.

Tip: Spread the name of your book far and wide. It may generate an additional 10% sales when there are lots of hits on the search engines.

Videos.

What does videos have to do with selling eBooks? Well, until recently not very much. However, lately there is a new marketing concept opening up.

Do keep in mind that Audio-Visual is the best of any form of marketing. It has been so for more than a century and it will remain so for time to come. Make a short video about your book. It does not matter what kind of book or what the contents is. Think of your book in terms of video – and make one. Yes, I admit; it is sometimes easier said than done. After all, I still experience a block about my 'eBook Guide', but it will come. Or, maybe it indicates to me the book is not a good option. Maybe I should change it completely.

How could I make a video? Honestly, now I am writing and I really have no clue what I am going to do for this book. My video for '*The Emerald Buddha*' is great and for the first book in this series – not too bad.

A few points to consider. Please, please do NOT start your video with the boring 'Hallo, my name is Corrie and I am here to tell you about....' gosh, how boring. Get it off, right away, big bang. Start with anything else but that antique!

Keep your video less than 2 minutes, a bit more than 1 minute at least. Make sure the clips, photos, voices and sound/music you are using in your video are not restricted or copyrighted. That will bang your video right off cyberspace.

That said, there are some very easy programs you can use, many free. MS-Windows has their easy to learn 'Moviemaker'. If you are more experienced, there are advanced software like 'DaVinci Revolve' also for free. Another on-line one, easy to use is http://www.wevideo.com/ or you can try the comical on-line free giff maker http://gifmaker.me/video-maker/.

Make a video and post it in Video websites, primarily www.youtube.com in the first book of this series we talked about making your Gmail account. Now that same name and password gives you access to YouTube with 15 minute per video upload time and unlimited space. Other good places to use are www.dailymotion.com and www.vimeo.com There are many more, but these are the main ones.

When you upload your video – you need keywords. Good keywords, good search results. And the more people can see your video, the more they might be interested in your book.

Yet, that is not the end. Upload or at least link that video to and in your book page on your website. In some book stores there is also an option to place a video right there on your books page; or in your Authors page.

People are hundred times more likely to watch a video than read a written add promotion. Do keep your short video interesting, captivating. Make the viewer get a desire to read your book for more information.

If you really struggle to start, get onto Google and search for images with your high level keywords. Pick a few of those images and string them together as your video, add some text and sound – and post it. You can also use clippings from other videos. Just get the story of your book out there in the Whole Wide World.

Tip 1: Nearly all (if not all) videos on YouTube are 'Creative Commons" licenced. In other words, you can legally use them, or clips from them, to make your own videos.

Tip 2: YouTube is now part of the Google corporate. Thus, great search engine advantage to post videos there. In addition, I notice a few weeks ago that YouTube has a good tool for making and/or editing your videos. Right there, on line, easy and fast.

Search Engines.

Goodness me, how the world changed. Gone are the days where you had to go to each and every Search Engine and actually list your website there. Literally inviting their robot to come and scan your website. You had to manually and physically type in the meta-tags, keywords, etc. Laborious, frustrating et all and then you wait a week or a month before you see your website listed.

Now-a-days, thanks to Google, those search engines are so advanced, they smell your new post or website or book or anything the moment you post it on the World Wide Web. I have been surprised a few times to see how quickly I get my new post listed in Google. A little slower with Yahoo and even slower with Bing. But we are talking of minutes, not months.

If you are just posting your book on an eBook store, there are a few things you can do to get an edge over the competitor.

1. The best-suited, key worded title.
2. The most powerful high value keywords in your sub-title.
3. The highest value keywords, phrases and long-tail keywords.
4. Make sure, when your book is posted on its page and you get the confirmation from the bookstore – you go to that page and look whatever link options there are possible. Link to your Author page, your other books, your website, the books video. Use everything possible.

The more places you post the 'good-keyword-name' of your book, the more it will appear amongst the results of any search engine. If your book title is only present in one website, then the listings in the search engines will only have one result. Post the title, sub-title in a hundred websites and you will have more than a hundred links in the search result. The more results, the more likely for people to notice them.

Yes, even have links within your book text. That does not always work, everywhere – though lately I see more and more eBook reading devices are completely adoptable to that. Regardless, the Search Engine will see them.

Search engines love linked references. Thus if my book itself has no internal or external links and your book links to 20 chapters inside the book and ten external links – then your book is going to get a much higher listing in the search engine results than mine.

You can use this to 'hijack' the potential reader even before he lands in the bookstore. Many of the smaller shops around the world actually rely on Search Engines to operate within their websites!

Recently I read an interesting article about 'Speak in Search Engine' where the author promotes the idea that search engines has their own language. To expand much on that now will be way beyond the scope of this book, you can research on it.

What I would like to point out is one particular aspect of that 'search engine language'. With the number of actual websites (registered active domain names) around the world now surpassing 1.1 billion – and then not even counting sub-domains and pages per website – the potential for search engines to find the exact required information becomes very intense.

What that article went on to explain is the usage of applicable phrases. Rather than typing 'dreams' as a search I should type 'sell dreams' – which will then give me more relevant results.

These are two key phrases you can use for doing more research about this critical 'language'. Keep this in mind when you determine your keywords.

Time permitting; I will include that in one of my future books for this series "Sell Your Dreams ~ Content Ideas".

Google: *'search engine structured data'* and *'SEO keyword structure'*.

Social Media

Do you want to know the absolute truth?

Social media is a complete waste of time for selling your eBook. Please say amen.

Yes, I do agree, there is some value in using various social media platforms; for a purpose. But as marketing tool to get lots of sale that just does not happen. Let me rephrase, Social Media is a good marketing tool if your aim is to get the value of about US$ 1 per twenty-hours spend working on that marketing platform.

To put that in perspective, you can rather spend 20-working hours on writing a complete new book, edit and publish it. See the first book in this series "*Sell your Dreams*" if you don't think you can do it in such short time frame.

Using Social Media for marketing, well that means you will need to post every day, a few times per day. I have a reasonable Facebook page, and another for my eBooks. On my main page I have at present something like 380 'Friends' and followers. Not all of them are posting, and not all of their posts comes to my Home Page either; else I will get some 300 to 500 posts per day to read! As it is, those posts I make is quickly pushed down the list on my friend's Home Pages. I know this because I actually have two Facebook Pages, the one follows the other. So I can see how quickly my own posts fades into obscurity.

When I started writing, I promoted my books heavily on Facebook, Twitter, LinkedIn, Pin-It, Hub Pages, etc. From a total of more than 1,000 people all over, I might have sold 10 book copies of three book titles in a six month period.

Hey, I even had 'Sell your Dreams' first book on for a two week period – for FREE. "Just go to my website and register your eMail address and you will receive the book for free". Guess what – that yielded me a wonderful total of 12 registrations!

And, yes – I did use paid promotions like "Boost your Post" and "Promote your Page". All that money; I would have more fun – and probably sales - by going to drink coffee in a shop and talking to people.

There is some value to use:

Yes, that is also true. Use it as a 'Notification Platform' is OK. Keep in contact with your readers. Tell them more about things you might not have included in the book. Especially when it comes to Non-Fiction. Tell them what you do, about writing your next book. Make friends with your readers is a good idea.

But there is a limit. Do NOT waste too much time on Social Media. Rather go relax, work in the garden or watch a video about something you might write about. Get ideas.

I have noticed that busy people, people that has a purpose – and those that has some money to spend on reading a book; these are very little on Social Media! They will rather read a book. You will rather get their business when you spend more time on your keywords and 'sub-luminal' marketing.

Most people will not believe me. Make a point of checking how many hours you spend on social chatting and what results you get. Compare that to what it takes to write a book and market it well. See where the differences are.

As relaxing, passing time and maybe prompting a bit about your book – yes, it is good. As tool for generating income – very bad, low paying option.

Off course, you can better apply your time in building a website; and use that to promote you and your books on Facebook. Just for that extra one or two sales per month.

Another good use is to post on Social Media with a link to your book where it is for sale. Search Engines picks that up – and you have an extra listing in their results.

Website.

Is a website for my books important? Yes. And no. Much depends on you and how you like to do things.

The first thing you need to realize is that building and maintaining a website does take a LOT of time. The best type of website is where you do have your books, each on their own page with all the relevant details; and best sales options.

Use your website as primary marketing tool for your eBook. Marketing is not sales – it is awareness.

Book store = 80% Sales, 20% marketing.

Website = 95% Marketing, 5% sales.

Let me give you another good example to understand. You see it all the way down the road. 'Coca Cola' = Marketing. '7Eleven' = Sales. Your website is the 'Coca Cola' billboard. Your Bookstore is your '7Eleven' or whatever *shop around the corner you have in your country'*.

Off course, you can use your website to sell your book directly – for those few extra dollars; but do not expect massive sales. Hopefully you can set your website up in such way that sales are all done automatically – quite a challenge and not so free anymore.

I am writing articles. Purely because I like the writing. For a long time I use to write about many things on Facebook, Hub-Pages, Pinterest, etc. but whatever I wrote faded to obscurity in days, if not hours. Then I started my Website, based on a Blog. Now I can write my articles, post them on my website – and from there it is automatically distributed to a few of my social media pages.

Typically it will take me an hour to write the article and post it. It will be placed in five social media pages within seconds, click per button. I am done. Gone back to writing or do something else.

You will need to continuously update on your Website. This is VERY important – else forget this notion. The more you expand on your personal website, with links, references, regular updates and all – the better ranking you can get on search engines like Google, Bing, etc.

Of course, the moment you see the words "Search Engine" you need to have big bells ringing – KEYWORDS.

Now, here is where you can ride the Tsunami of waves with the marketing of your eBook. IF you understand the working of Search Engines, ranking systems and the Art of the Keywords as I explained above.

On the page of each book, you should make extensive use of keywords. There is basically no limit on the number of keywords you can and should use – provided they are present in the content of that page. In addition to this, the number of outside links you have on that page also boost your Search Engine rankings.

As basic concept for this book. There will be the normal items like the Cover page image, a write up about the book, price, some promotions, etc. Then I will link this book to every book seller I wish. I will create a video, which will be linked and embedded on the books page. I will provide links on the page for each link which I refer to in the book. I will mention the actual name of the book as often as possible, with a link back to this same page. And I will link to other interesting articles about the main subject of my book – but always open in a new window!

When the page is scanned by the Search engine they should find:

A list of keywords and key phrases.
All embedded in the page.
Plenty of links.
Graphic Image(s).
Video Content.
References to big sites i.e. your book store.

The result? Since 'Sell your Dreams' is new on the market, I will refer to my older eBook 'The Emerald Buddha'. Google yields 51,000 results and my book is listed as second result. First after a Google Paid Add.

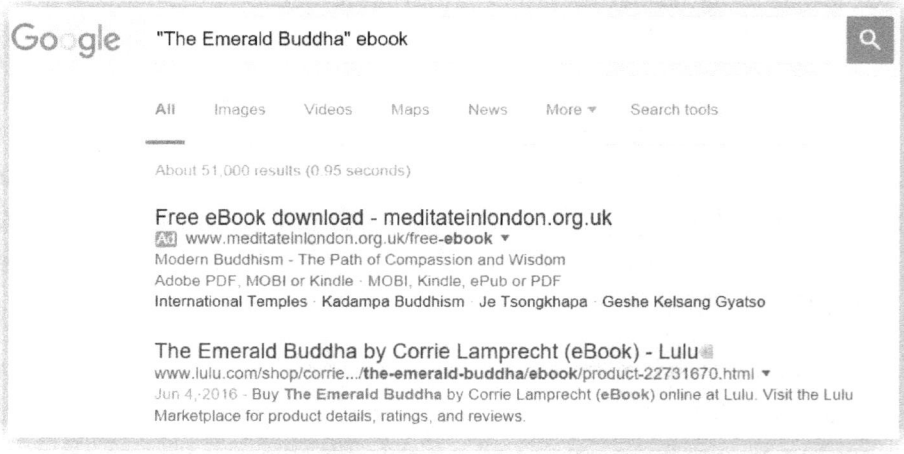

Say for argument sake I was looking for an image related to my search, so I will tell Google to only give me images. Then this is the result.

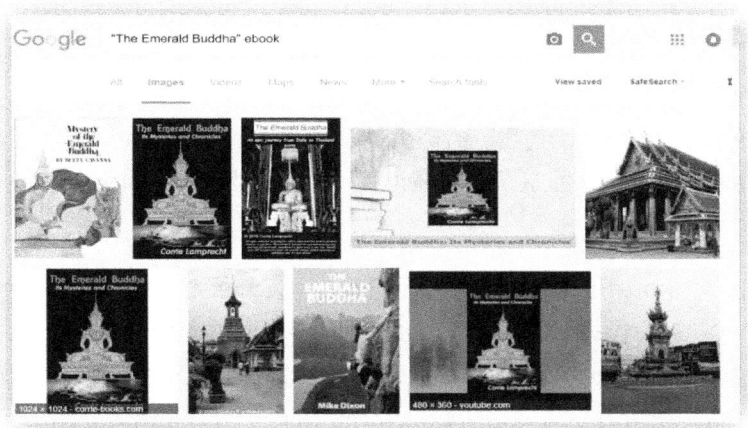

Right there on the first page of the images, amongst the first two lines are FIVE images of this book. They all refer to different websites! Amazon, Smashwords, Dailymotion, #5 is my own webpage "www.corrie-books.com" and #6 my own YouTube Channel. Scrolling further down on this First Page are seven more images of this book. In addition there is one photo of me as author and one about the link to my website for my second book 'eBook Guide' in which I refer to 'The Emerald Buddha' a few times.

The same search but opt for videos, the results on page one with 13 listings there are five referring to the videos about my eBook. Remember the chapter about Videos explaining how to promote your book and website.

Typing just an open search on Google with the free keywords – emerald Buddha, there are 1.4 million results – with my book listed on page 5. Not bad. Nearly all of the listings before my book was in reference to the great tourist attraction - Emerald Buddha Temple in Bangkok. I have to admit, being a bit busy in this last three months – I did not really attend to marketing that book very well – yet. And my website is only on-line since two months ago! The results is quite astonishing, even to me.

You should also create a Comments section on your page where visitors can leave remarks, comments, questions and reviews about your book. That will help boosting your website a lot.

Keywords, links and cross-linking. Use your website as primary platform to do marketing on Search Engines and promoting yourself and your books. It is a powerful tool with lots of freedom to apply everything you learned in this book.

As for website; there are two targets. First to get people to visit your site and second to get them subscribing. Get their email address into your list. If you have a selected list of say 5,000 people reading or interested in your books, you may get 2,000 copies sold shortly after every new book launch. More important, these are your most likely source for ratings and reviews on your books.

Email.

To use e-mails as a form of direct marketing is an absolute 100% waste of time. Maybe from 5,000 emails you might get one sale – if you are not completely blacklisted as a spammer.

However, if you have subscribers and you keep them informed – then this is a very useful tool. Subscriber e-mails are 70% effective.

Offer free newsletters to subscribers. Once a month you send them an update. Write not only books, but also keep a blog and write some articles. Make the newsletter interesting – and related to the books you are publishing.

If you do get an e-mail from a fan or reader of one of your books – you MUST reply. Do not make people feel upset, discarded or ignored.

Post the name.

Promote, promote, promote. It is all part of the marketing game. Get the name of your book out there. The more platforms you can have it magically appear on, the better. But – remain related. It is no good to promote your Surfing book on a page for Retirement Villages!

The more your name and that of your book are in the face of potential buyers, the better – but do NO SPAM.

This kind of marketing is tertiary – third class. But, if you have a few spare minutes, why not? First do make sure your On-site bookstore is loaded to the maximum, your website is jammed and above all – your Search Engine issues like keywords, title, links, etc. are absolutely optimized.

<u>Some options to consider.</u>

Place a copy or a poster of your book behind you when you do other on-line things like talking on Skype or messenger.

Refer to your book whenever and wherever you can, but be subtle.

You can hold some conferences or on-line Question time about your book, if you wish.

Get Reviews.

There are honest reviews and there is big cheating. I am not interested in the cheating ones, so, here are some ideas for honest reviews.

In general, the rule is that you as Author are not allowed to review your own book, neither any family members living in the same house. People are not (supposed) to be remunerated in any way in exchange for reviews. It is supposed to be only a true reader, but on all bookstores, I noticed that anybody could review any other book, regardless weather he has actually read it. Whatever let me explain the rather honest, true, above all rules, review.

The reader that just read your book. Studies have found that in general less than 3% of the readers will do the effort to go back to where they purchased your book and actually write a review.

There is a method that does yield good results. On the last page of your book, before the 'About Author' or other book promotions – add a request. As example, you can look at the last page of this book.

Believe me, this does make your reader feel good, they are on the brink of becoming your new best friend; or maybe you will become their best-friend-author. Most people love the feeling of 'being wanted, being appreciated'.

Strategy.

1. You can write your book first. Alternatively, a good strategy is to research the genre and keywords first. That might help to outline your book.

2. Research your Title and Sub-Title. Make sure each and every word are powerful and easy searchable.

3. Start your 'Blanket Promotions' – use the subluminal techniques.

4. Remember the 'Back Page' promotions. That is where you sell your older books and where you already start promoting your next book.

5. Remember to invite people – with a link to your book's page – to place a review. Above all – promote yourself. Link to your website; get e-mail addresses to your list.

6. When your book is done, cover page and all; then get ready to post on-line.

7. Select the most suitable category or categories to list your book into.

8. Enter your keywords in the order of importance. Keep in mind the option to use additional niche names as keywords.

9. Make a video and link it to your book and webpage.

10. If you are so inclined and have lots of little free times; then make posts to your Social Media.

11. Keep track of how your book is doing. Once a week, once a month or so. If sales are down, then consider to change the Category, or change the Cover Page, or change the Keywords – or change all of the above. Keep an eye on your keywords performance on Search Engines.

12. Always keep your eyes open for additional ways to promote your book. Maybe there are site discounts from the bookstore?

13. The lucky number. For each of my books, I create a special sub-directory on my computer – and I have at least two external backups. Can you imagine losing your hard work? I have been there. Twice.

14. In that directory for my book is a file which I call "(book_name) - MetaData". At first when I publish my eBook all relevant data is written there. Including also the searches I did for keywords, phrases and categories. Later it might be helpful to review and see where the people 'moved'. I keep record of whatever I do with that book. Here is a sample cutting from the "The Emerald Buddha" file.

I have everything there. Use the same information for every place you post your book. In return, I also have the links for the book, promotion videos, etc. Very easy to pull out, copy ad past whenever I need it.

LINK ADDRESSES:

Amazon.com – ASIN = B01BLR3VQ0   (Updated 4 July 2016)
Link: https://www.amazon.com/Emerald-Buddha-Its-Mysteries-Chronicles-ebook/dp/B01BLR3VQ0

CreateSpace.com -   https://www.createspace.com/6394852
ISBN-13: 978-1535067515
ISBN-10: 1535067519
Black and White (Grey scale) print   - My cost US$ 2.15
                                          - Sales   US$ 14.95

METADATA:

Title: The Emerald Buddha
Sub-Title: Its Mysteries and Chronicles
Author: Corrie Lamprecht
Publisher: Cornelius Lamprecht
Price: US$ 5.99

Short Description: (Not in Amazon)
One of the most valuable relics of the world is housed on the grounds of the Royal Palace in Bangkok. The Emerald Buddha has indeed a very interesting history, stretching over more than 2,060 years.

Long Description: (Amazon is up to 4,000 characters)
In the Royal Palace of Bangkok is one of the most revered Buddhist images, of the entire world. More than three million people visit that temple every year. It was the original master of most Buddhist images carved in later centuries around South East Asia.

The bottom line? Get traffic – to your book listing and to your website. Convert them to subscribers. Make the subscriber a friend of fan. Your mail list is your rocket launcher to space.

Back Page.

Please review: <u>Sell Your Dreams ~ Effective Book Marketing</u>

Below is an image with four of the books in this series. I wanted to update them, but decided to rather leave for this book as is.

You will see there are changes in the Sub-Titles, I made these after I did a more intensive research on my categories and keywords. Actually I spend two full days just to review all four these books 'metadata' and shifting them to other categories. On both books, since I made the changes during this past week – there is a remarkable increase in sales. Not enough yet!

Sell Your Dreams
Get Your Money

Corrie Lamprecht

Introduction

This is probably the shortest book I will ever write. Yet, for selling your books and get the maximum money back into your own pocket, this is the most valuable book. If you apply a few simple guidelines, this book may pay for itself within the first ten books you sell.

Most of the bigger eBook stores are based in the USA. The US government needs every cent they can possibly get. If you are selling your books, on line through those bookstores – it is considered taxable in the USA. Regardless from where you are and where you pay your taxes – you will suffer from a 30% withholding tax on all your eBook sales. Unless . . .

That is only the start of some difficulty any person from outside of the US suffers. There are also other issues. Being paid could be another obstacle. Amazon for instance does not work with PayPal or any other similar payment systems. Therefore, they will send you a cheque by mail which you will need to put in your bank. Now, I do not know much about all the rest of the world, but I can assure you that will be a very sad story in South Africa, at least.

This book is extremely valuable for any writer outside of the USA.

Read on, I hope you will benefit from this e-Book and welcome to the rapidly expanding group of non-U.S.A. writers, publishers – and readers!

Just Imagine.

I finished writing my very well researched book "*The Emerald Buddha*" in January 2016. I did a lot of research, verified my facts, painstakingly synchronized it all, and typed it out at average 20-words per minute. Then I had an English Teacher friend going over it for language and spelling and grammar and whatever other mistakes. Fixed that, did the formatting and all. The formatting took me a full month. I was ready. Logged onto Amazon.com where I was going to rake in the millions, ready to publish.

Dunk. They want my bank account details. However, none of the banks I am using was acceptable. What is going on here? Eventually, no they are not doing direct deposits or transfers to banks outside of the USA. They only send cheques. Actual paper cheques by land mail! In this modern time, I thought such ancient methods are no more in use. You know the old story of "*The cheque is in the mail*". Well, the problem for places like Indonesia, India and South Africa – it is very strange to get your mail at all.

OK, I tried to get my PayPal account in operation. Nope, Amazon does not work with PayPal. The only way I could be paid; is a cheque by snail mail. Now, I really did think I will sell many books, but I also realized it would not shoot off to the moon in the first few months. What to do?

I could just imagine walking into my bank here in Thailand with a massive $6.40 royalty cheque from the USA. Hey, do you realize there are clearance fees, bank charges and it will take three weeks at least? Stupid Farang. Poor me, of all my hard work and the nice income from all my book sales and by the end of the day I will only remain with a very small portion.

Little did I realize then that there is another big nightmare around the corner. The US Revenue Service – in short, the Tax Man. He is going to eat another 30% before Amazon creates my cheque payment.

Oh well, that is it. Let us move on to other dealers. Hmmm. All of the good and bigger ones are in the USA. There are only a very few reasonable ones outside in the rest of the world, not really worth it to go for them either. I was stuck.

Nevertheless, I was determined. The results of weeks of research are here in this short book for you.

I trust it will save you a lot of frustration and time.

Other Book Stores

Well, the first and only option I could get around this was to publish my books on other bookstores. In particular then, in bookstores outside the sphere of the US Tax influence. I set of on searching. Yes, I did find a few. Mostly in the UK region, few in Europe two in Australia, but none are strong. Nearly all of those tax departments do indeed claim a stake on your cake, in particular with General Sales Tax and Value Added Tax.

There is a simple mathematic equation. If you have a million products to compete with, you definitely want more than a million potential customers. In addition to that, you are selling a book for a low price of say US$ 3.00. You definitely do not only want to sell one book per month. When I do my market research, I learned from those intelligent people that the average eBook buyer is buying around 1.7 books per month.

Ahhh, I found Lulu.com. Then there is the big SmashWords.com and Barnes & Noble. Do not forget about Kobo. I investigated 27 of these stores intensively. Together, they are raking in less than 20% of the eBook world sales. The rest is . . . yes, Amazon.com. Damn, what can I do?

The good news was that most of them do work with PayPal. Thus, I went ahead and opened my accounts, posted my book and felt very happy that all was possible at last. I saw that Smashwords would even post my book on Amazon.com, free. The same with some 17 other bookstores where they will place my book. A nice 'One-Stop-Service'. WOW, this is great. Happily, I got on with writing my second book "eBook Guide".

Then I waited and I watched. One morning I got an email from Smashwords. I have sold one copy of the Emerald Buddha. Sold another two during the next day. I was so happy, so excited. I could not even sit on a chair. But, how much did I earn?

Crash! Back to Earth. A stunning US$ 1.28 per book by the time the money hit in PayPal. WHAT? I thought I will get at least US$ 2.70. That was when I learned about The Taxman. The American Tax Man.

This was getting ridiculous. I had to get around it. It was just the kind of thing I am usually good at. Thus, I went digging. That is enough said about the run-in. Let us go on to the answers.

Financial

Credit / Debit Card.

Off course, the easiest way is to use your Credit Card or sometimes even debit cards. In all cases there is a risk concerning your bank account and personal information that can land in the wrong hands. Mostly the booksellers do not deposit money to your Credit Card accounts anyway.

Some banks allow you to create a temporary or Virtual Credit Card based account to use on-line. This is in my opinion the best and safest way to do it. You will need to find out from your bank about this option (*Currently, exclusively a VISA product*). If your bank does not offer this service, check with other banks around your home location.

Only one of my banks in Thailand has this option. It is my personal favourite, and most secure, Internet banking to use.

PayPal:

PayPal is an on-line type of banking system, which you can use to pay for safe on-line (internet) shopping and to get money into your account if you are selling something. It was part of the eBay stable – hence the problem with some vendors not wanting to use PayPal. They are direct competition and never want to share their customer's data with the competition.

Most of the bookstores do work with PayPal. It is the most versatile and widely used trading facility; I would recommend you to open an account there. It is easy; you need all your own information like name, address, etc. In addition, you will need a Bank Account that can link to PayPal. Not all banks do. If you do not have, then you should consider opening another bank account with a bank that does work with PayPal. In Thailand, I have accounts at five different banks. Only three of them are PayPal friendly.

There are various ways to get money into your PayPal account, either by direct bank transfer or by using a Credit Card.

Register at: www.paypal.com
Need personal info, email address and bank details.
Usually takes less than 24 hours from apply to get using.

On-Line Electronic Bank.

Then there is a third option. You can create an On-Line bank account. Completely Internet based, with the minimum fuss. Personally, I like this option for its safety and ease of use - it is perfect. However, I prefer not to keep a big balance sleeping there! For people living in crime ridden South Africa or insecure places like India and Kenya – this is an excellent, relatively safe prospect.

I created an On-Line bank account in the USA while sitting at my computer in Thailand. It took about 15 minutes until all was set and ready to go. My account was with PaYoneer Bank. See the about Payoneer below.

There are an ever-increasing number of on-line banks popping up all over the world. Here is a short list of such banks. Since I am happy with Payoneer, I did not use any of these myself. Thus, all I can do is to give you their names and possible links. You should investigate carefully before you trust your millions to them!

Scotia Bank - http://www.scotiabank.com

HSBC - http://www.hsbc.co.uk

ICICI Bank - http://www.icicibank.com

PaYoneer: - www.payoneer.com

This is my personal choice of on-line banking, especially with the payments of royalties. I am using PaYoneer, I have tested their system – and to date they are running smoothly for me.

If you want to consider and sign up for Payoneer - please use the link above, or if it is not working, there is also one on my website page for this book, it will earn me some much needed referral fee! In addition, once you had a US$ 100 turnover in your account, (if it is a referred account) – you will also get US$ 25 as a gift.

Payoneer is not just an on-line money trader, it is a full featured financial business and in my personal opinion, the best Internet related financial operative, at the present. Payoneer was founded in 2005 and provides for freelancers and freelance marketplaces; with all the tools, they need to pay and be paid – as if locally.

"Payoneer provides cross-border wire transfers, online payments, and a refillable debit card service for businesses and working professionals. Payoneer account holders have the option to receive funds into their local bank account or e-wallet, or via a re-loadable prepaid debit card, which is issued through MasterCard and can be used at ATMs or at the point-of-purchase. As of 2015, Payoneer is available in more than 100 currencies in 200 countries with 3+ million users."

Practically, what it means is that with Payoneer you have a local bank account in 200 countries – including the USA. That means your money from any eBook seller (and any other on-line sales) can be directly deposited to your 'local' bank. Different currencies, different locations. From there you can then either apply for and use their Debit Card – or transfer money to your local bank at minimal cost compared to any other such service I know about.

You can buy (expense) and sell (Income) directly from your Payoneer account. In my humble opinion – the best option for most on-line business operations; for now at least. If you live outside of the main centres and wish to sell your books on-line, I do recommend this feature. I linked two of my Thai Bank accounts to Payoneer in order to transfer money to and from those accounts. Currently Payoneer has a flat rate of US$ 2.99 per transaction in 55 countries and up to US$ 9.95 in other countries. Normally they maintain an exchange rate of 2% above Mid-Rate between buy and sell currencies.

Other potential banks:

Here is a link with a number of online only banks to explore. I have not checked any of them.

http://online-only-banks-review.toptenreviews.com/

With a normal Credit Card or some Debit Card, you can do on-line shopping, easy. However, you cannot withdraw any payments to your account. On top of that, I am a little careful about giving Credit /Debit card details on the Internet. Credit cards has a monthly/yearly maintenance cost.

The Tax Issue

Ahh, the Tax Man. He who eats unconditionally and never gives value in return. I hate to pay them a lot of money, hence this special section – for those outside of the U.S.A. and their 30% withholding tax greed.

If your book is sold in the USA – you will pay 30% withholding tax in the USA. If your book is sold through a US company, you will pay 30% withholding tax. If your book is bought by somebody in Fiji and you stay in the Maldives; but the transaction is done at Aamazon.com – which is U.S.A. based; you will pay 30% withholding tax. So what is the answer?

Try NOT to sell your book through the USA. Rather try to sell it at another store outside of the USA. Amazon.com for instance does have stores in the USA, United Kingdom, Spain, France, Germany, Italy, Netherland, Japan, Brazil, Mexico, Australia and India. Unfortunately, this is only valid if people are physically buying from those countries; and the bookseller is non-USA.

The same comes into play with other eBook stores. Most often, you cannot control the buyer or sales location. However, remember you are doing most of the marketing, and that might not be exclusively Amazon.com. Make sure your book published in some stores outside of the USA, is at least.

The only other store I will recommend to use, completely outside of the USA is Kobo.com. They are the second biggest dealer, physical present in many countries around the world with affiliates – and they are a Canadian company. Thus, no problems with the US Withholding tax issue.

Here is the Tsunami of Truth. If you want to increase your potential sales - by at least 80% - you need to be on

Amazon.com for your eBook and CreateSpace.com for your paper book. Fortunately, there is a way to either reduce or maybe eliminate this 30% US Withholding tax. Presently it seems to work fine for me, but nothing is ever guaranteed, and it might not be too easy.

In Amazon, you should complete the Form W-8BEN (*Certificate of Foreign Status of Beneficial Owner for United States Tax Withholding*). If this is done right and approved, your Withholding tax will be on a reduced scale. Do the same for every place you post your books, even CreateSpace needs a separate form.

For Amazon.com, go to https://kdp.amazon.com/help?topicId=AFIB5T5Q85C7J and follow the instructions.

1: Your full real name (do not use a pen name here!)

2: Your country of citizenship (They might require a copy of ID)

3: Permanent physical residence address in your country; not P.O.Box.

4: Mailing address if other than Permanent Address.

5: US SSN or ITIN – Leave empty if you are not US Resident.

6: Your Tax number in your country of residence.

7: Reference number – if some other application

8: Date of Birth

9: The country where you are citizen and/or Permanent Residence if not the same.

10. The Treaty details you wish to apply for, normally just leave blank.

Signature: Amazon has the arrangement for Electronic signature of this form, which you can follow. Else, you need to download and send by mail. Sign your name and enter the date signed. Be sure to put the date in the U.S. format of MM/DD/YYYY.

Here is the basic list of Countries and the percentage of Withholding taxes they will deduct, if your Form W8-BEN is accepted.

Australia: 5%, Austria: 0%, Bangladesh: 10%, Barbados: 5%, Belgium: 0%, Bulgaria: 5%, Canada: 0%, China: 10%, Cyprus: 0%, Czech Republic: 0%, Denmark: 0%, Egypt: 15%, Estonia: 10%, Finland: 0%, France: 0%, Germany: 0%, Greece: 0%, Hungary: 0%, Iceland: 0%, India: 15%, Indonesia: 10%, Ireland: 0%, Israel: 10%, Italy: 0%, Jamaica: 10%, Japan: 0%, Kazakhstan: 10%, South Korea: 10%, Latvia: 10%, Lithuania: 10%, Luxemburg: 0%, Malta: 10%, Mexico: 10%, Morocco: 10%, Netherlands: 0%, New Zealand: 5%, Norway: 0%, Pakistan: 0%, Philippines: 15%, Poland: 10%, Portugal: 10%, Romania: 10%, Russia: 0%, Slovakia: 0%, Slovenia: 5%, South Africa: 0%, Spain: 5%, Sri Lanka: 10%, Sweden: 0%, Switzerland: 0%, Thailand: 5%, Trinidad & Tobago: 0%, Tunisia: 15%, Turkey: 10%, Ukraine: 10%, United Kingdom: 0%, Venezuela: 10%

Why not sell directly?

Yes, this is a great option. Besides, except for the bank transaction fees, you will keep all the income. It is relative easy to set up for selling your books directly. But.

The most important BUT in all of this is that you need to consider your options. In case you post on Amazon.com for instance, it is on and done. You do not need to pamper or attend at all. You are free to go away – or keep on writing your next books. IF you do go the way of direct marketing and sales from your own platform – you freedom is caged in. You will need to check your flow, actions and problems all the time.

You will do a LOT of work and you will really need to do a lot of marketing. That on its own might not cost much in money, but it will eat severely on your time. At the end of the day, unless you are a magician-like Guru – your sales will be about the same as 10% of your mailing list. Most people I tracked have a mailing list of between 500 and 10,000 names. Thus, their direct sales are probably not more than 50 to 1,000 books, over all.

Yes, their income is at least 20% more per book sale. You need to ask yourself if this is a good option for you. Unless you plan to write many books, at least 5 per year, it is not a viable option. The bottom line is also that this way will probably not get you more than 5% of the Amazon potential in sales.

That said there are many options to consider. I will not go in full details since there are plenty of videos and free writings to read more details.

Option 1 - Own Website:

Create a website. I recommend a low cost hosting site that is using WordPress as creation software. Wix, GoDaddy,

WpNode, x10Hosting, Btehost and many more. Just Google them or "*Free web hosting*".

I register my domain name and renting web space at 'Inmotionhosting.com'. The total package cost me around US$ 120 per year but there are a number of different reasons for me to go this expensive.

Option 2 - The Google Road:

The next is just an example; you can use many other options, including running your own complete website. These are nearly free options.

Register for Gmail.com (eMail address). Get 15 Gb free Cloud storage. Upload your book to the Google Drive. Copy the URL code and keep it one side. Next, you register on a Commercial site like www.stripe.com and let them handle your commercial part.
Then you are off to sell your book, anywhere, even on Facebook. Pay 2.9% +US$ 0.30 per sale only.

You can also create a small website on Google sites and use a button from PayPal for direct sales. There are many info and videos available. You will probably need to use a few features combined like Google Sites, Google Cloud, Google Forms and an auto mailer like Mailchimp.

Please do register on my website for the monthly News Letter since I will keep on posting updates there, in particular about this Google options. Google is busy with a whole set of new developments, which will be very useful for self-publishing authors.

Option 3 – The Facebook Concept:

This is a brand new potential. Create a Facebook Page and there are options to implement a PayPal button, though you might need to ship your book by yourself on this stage.

The E-Junkie Road – and others: (http://www.e-junkie.com/)

Depending on which server you use, there is sometimes a monthly fee, sometimes a percentage of your sales. In the case of E-Junkie, for US$ 5.00 per month flat rate, you can upload up to 10 product in up to 50Gb. Get a 'button' and go sell, anywhere, anytime. Be it on your website or Social Media. Let them handle all the sales and shipping of your digital book. This is nearly a fully automated system, good option. Just one shortcoming, they are not doing your marketing like Amazon.

See: http://www.hongkiat.com/blog/services-sell-digital-products/ for more options.

Strategy and Consider

In my humble opinion, selling on Amazon.com is the best option for making many sales and generates a good income. If you are outside of the USA, I recommend adding Kobo.com and promote that link as your primary sales.

Doing your direct sales, website, Google and mailing – the way I am doing now – is good for long term planning. Maybe. I am currently working at least 70% of my time on other sales platforms and maintaining the website.

Frankly, I am not even sure it is going to be worth the efforts. Maybe it would be better just to write more books and attend more on the issues I described in my previous book of this series – Effective Book Marketing.

I wish you a great success.

Please do subscribe on my website for updates.

Do not forget to give me a review and comment! I truly need it.

Back Page

Dear Reader,

I hope you have enjoyed this book and above all, that you find it of value.

The bookstore where you bought the book (or my website) has a feature for customers to post a review. All such product reviews are important to the author, the marketplace and other potential customers.

Could I kindly ask from you this very big favour.

Would you spare a minute and write a review for me. Please?

We do appreciate all reviews, positive and negative. I trust that if you are not happy with this product, you will give me some constructive comments included in your review. If you are reasonably happy, it is a great motivation for me as writer to continue on this tenuous path.

I will try to post a direct link to this book's page and also to my Authors Page if that is available. You might be lucky to just click on the link below – else you need to go through your normal log- in.

In gratitude.
Corrie Lamprecht

Please do subscribe on my website for the monthly newsletter and updates.

http://www.corrie-books.com

About the Author

Facebook.

www.ingramcontent.com/pod-product-compliance
Lightning Source LLC
Chambersburg PA
CBHW060621290526
45793CB00001B/96